BEGINNER'S GUIDE TO SELLING ANTIQUES ON ETSY

BY ANN ECKHART

INTRODUCTION

In 2005, I was working at the local Chamber of Commerce, feeling burnt out and yearning to become my own boss. After exploring several options, I decided to start a home-based gift basket business, leveraging my business connections to cater to corporate clients. In invested in gift baskets and fillers such as food, candles, and coffee mugs, and enjoyed the process of creating themed baskets.

Sales were steady until summer arrived, and business came to a standstill. With no holidays and many people on vacation, I found myself sitting on a heap of gift basket supplies and inventory, including food that had expiration dates.

To clear my inventory and make some cash, I contemplated listing some items for sale on eBay. However, the thought of selling online, especially on an auction platform, was nerve-wracking. Back then, EBay was the only option for people to sell goods online, and Amazon was still primarily selling books. While it's hard to imagine these days, back in 2005 the only online shopping websites were EBay and Amazon.

Despite my reservations, I decided to take the plunge and list some items for sale on EBay. This was my first attempt at selling anything online, and I had no idea what to expect. To my surprise, the items I listed sold immediately. I began to gradually add more of my excess inventory to the site until I had depleted my supplies.

I was so excited about how quickly I had liquidated my inventory that I immediately started exploring other products that my gift basket suppliers offered that I could sell on eBay. Some of the products I found were standalone gifts such as coffee mugs, teapots, books, and plush toys. I ordered these items in small batches to test them out, and they would sell as soon as I listed them.

By the end of 2005, I had given up on selling gift baskets and shifted my focus entirely to selling gift items on eBay. When Amazon opened up its platform to third-party sellers, I jumped at the opportunity and started selling there as well. My sales skyrocketed, and I was thrilled with the results! For four years, I enjoyed a steady stream of amazing Amazon sales, with my eBay sales adding an extra boost to my income.

As they say, however, all good things must come to an end. After six years of selling online, the competition had finally caught up. More and more people were starting to sell on both eBay and Amazon, and even some of my wholesale suppliers started to sell directly to the public. To add to that, numerous stores were opening their own e-commerce websites. I was no longer one of a handful of online sellers, but rather one of millions. As quickly as my online selling career had begun, it seemed to screech to a halt as I found myself buried under the weight of competition.

Desperately seeking a way to save my business, I stumbled upon YouTube videos of people discussing how they found items at garage sales and thrift stores to sell online. I was familiar with antique dealers, of course, but I always assumed that they were people who had their own antique stores, sold in antique malls, or made the rounds at flea markets. However, these YouTube sellers were bypassing in-person sales entirely and selling their vintage collectibles on eBay and Etsy. I realized that this was the path to saving my business, and I began educating myself on vintage collectibles that I found at estate sales.

However, my transition from selling new wholesale gift items to secondhand antiques was not an overnight switch. I had a lot to learn about the vintage market, and while I already knew how to sell on eBay, I needed to learn how to sell on Etsy as well. Despite my years of experience, it felt as though I was starting my business from scratch.

Fortunately, I found Etsy's platform to be somewhat similar to eBay, so the photographing, listing, and shipping processes were fairly easy to learn. But there were significant differences in selling on Etsy, the most notable being the overall aesthetic of Etsy versus eBay. Etsy shoppers, I soon learned, had very different expectations than eBay shoppers.

On eBay, anything goes. As a seller, you can list a pair of used sneakers alongside a vintage figurine without anyone batting an eye. Customers on eBay search for the items they want and rarely look at the other listings a seller is offering.

On Etsy, however, sellers need to curate their shops. Etsy shoppers expect more than eBay buyers in terms of photographs, product selection, and packaging. And while eBay's search relies on keyword loaded listing title, Etsy's search relies heavily on Search Engine Optimization (SEO), a tedious task of repeating important keywords in not only the listing title but also in the description, tags, and shop sections. In short, Etsy's platform is "needier" than eBay's, and learning how to maximize my listings took time.

While adjusting to the higher expectations of Etsy shoppers presented a learning curve, I realized that it also gave me the potential to charge more for my items than I could on eBay. Unlike eBay shoppers who are always on the lookout for deals, Etsy buyers are looking for antiques to add to their collections or vintage treasures to give as gifts. They are willing to pay more for high-quality items, and they expect nothing but the best. Listing on Etsy takes a bit more care and thought, but the increased profits are worth the time.

In this book, I will be sharing with you everything I have learned about selling antiques on Etsy, including:

- Why you should sell your antiques on Etsy
- What antiques and vintage collectibles sell best on Etsy
- How to open an Etsy Shop
- Etsy SEO made easy
- Photography tips and tricks to present your products in the best way possible
- How to list your items on Etsy
- What shipping supplies you will need to run an Etsy shop
- How to process and ship Etsy orders
- How to deal with customer service issues
- How to manage your Etsy finances
- How to advertise your Etsy shop
- How to grow your Etsy business for maximum profits

Selling online, including on Etsy, is no longer limited to those with advanced technical skills. All you need is a computer, an internet connection, a camera, and a printer, and you're good to go. These days you can even photograph, list, and ship right from your smartphone. Reselling, as we call it, is the type of job that almost anyone can do.

However, it takes more than the right equipment to build a successful Etsy antique shop. You need to find the right products and present them in a way that will attract shoppers. Moreover, you need to provide excellent customer service to turn those shoppers into loyal customers and grow your business. An Etsy antique shop closely resembles a brick-and-mortar antique store: the more effort you put into cultivating your products and the aesthetic of your shop, the more successful you will be.

It may seem intimidating, but with the right guidance, you can achieve success on Etsy. I assure you that after reading this book, you will have the skills and knowledge to start making money selling antiques and vintage collectibles on Etsy.

So, if you're ready to take the plunge and start your Etsy antique shop, let's dive in and get started!

PRO TIP: "Antique dealers," "pickers," and "resellers" are all terms used to refer to people who buy and sell vintage collectibles. However, the most current term used is "reseller". And the job "resellers" perform is "reselling." Rarely do Etsy sellers refer to themselves as "antique dealers" or "pickers." In today's world, they are "resellers." So as you begin your journey of selling antiques on Etsy, you will want to refer to yourself as a "reseller," too!

CHAPTER ONE: WHY YOU SHOULD SELL YOUR ANTIQUES ON ETSY

Whether you are already an established antique dealer or a collector who wants to turn your hobby into a business, Etsy, alongside eBay, is the best place to sell vintage items. If you thought Etsy was only for selling crafts, this may surprise you. In fact, Etsy allows for the sale of items in three different categories:

1. Crafts such as handmade and homemade products
2. Supplies for making crafts and homemade products
3. Vintage collectibles

It is the third category of "vintage" that "antiques" fall under. The terms "vintage" and "antique" can be a bit confusing, however, as different people and industries have their own definitions of these terms. When it comes to selling on Etsy, Etsy has a specific definition of what qualifies as vintage, which is items that are at least 20 years old.

On the other hand, antiques are generally considered to be items that are at least 100 years old. Many people refer to anything old as an antique, hence why I named this book *Beginner's Guide To Selling Antiques On Etsy*, not *Selling Vintage*. Most people who claim they sell antiques are actually selling vintage. For that reason, using the term "antiques" makes me a bit uncomfortable as it isn't actually factual; but since it is currently the more popular term to describe vintage items, I will use "antique" throughout this book.

It's important to note that not everyone agrees on these definitions of "vintage" versus "antique." Some people, such as myself, actually think of vintage items as being at least 30 years old. However, when it comes to selling on Etsy, their guidelines of what constitutes "vintage" is 20 years old, and that is the only guideline they offer for sellers. There is no separate category for "antiques." If it's 20 years old, it's okay to sell it on Etsy in the "vintage" category. However, I still believe that you should only list an item as an "antique" if it is 100 years old.

Regardless of how you or your customers define "vintage" or "antique," when you sell on Etsy, you will be listing anything older than 20 years as "vintage." In a way this is nice as Etsy removes the debate for all of us: If the product you are listing for sale is at least 20 years old, it is considered "vintage." Not "modern" or "antique," just "vintage." End of debate.

But before we dive into selling antiques and vintage collectibles on Etsy, let's first talk about why you would even want to sell your items online in the first place. You may have a long history of selling at antique malls, flea markets, or perhaps even your own antique store. Selling locally and in person has its advantages. There is no photographing, listing, or shipping to do. And you don't have to worry about buyers who don't pay or difficult customer service issues such as lost packages. Many antique dealers I speak with shudder at the thought of selling online. They often cite a lack of computer skills as the number one reason along with a general fear of the unknown.

However, if you want to grow your business and make more money, moving some or all of your items online is the only way to do it. Selling online has several advantages, including:

Reaching a wider audience: How many shoppers typically attend antique shows and flea markets? How many shoppers visit antique malls and stores? And how many of these shoppers actually purchase anything?

"Antiquing" is somewhat of a hobby sport. People love to browse, but often they don't buy. However, online shoppers are buyers. They don't log on to Etsy to browse; they go to Etsy to buy. While you may lug the same items to show after show, year after year, without anyone so much as looking at most of what you are selling, when you list those same products online, you are putting your items in front of tens of millions of customers. You can sell to customers from all over the country, or even internationally, giving you a much better chance of finding the buyers willing to pay for what you are selling.

No displays to maintain: When you sell antiques online, you don't have to worry about the physical space limitations that come with selling at a flea market or antique mall. You can list as many items as you want without worrying about running out of booth space or display cases. While you do need to store the items you list for sale, you don't have to display them. Instead, you can use industrial shelving and totes to keep your inventory safe until it sells.

If you do sell in a physical store, you can keep your items for sale there but also list them online. Most dealers have more inventory than they can display for sale, so listing products online will help you move things faster. And if you sell at in-person events, you can advertise your Etsy shop to attendees by distributing business cards. This allows you to focus on the items you know you can move at in-person events while keeping more long-tail inventory listed on Etsy.

No time limitations: With an Etsy shop, you don't have to worry about being limited by the hours of operation of a flea market or antique mall. Your items are available for purchase 24/7, which means that customers can buy from you at any time of day or night. And while you will need to ship orders promptly, you aren't under pressure to get more items to your booth space. You can list what you want when you want.

Lower overhead costs: Selling antiques online typically involves lower overhead costs than selling them locally at a flea market or antique mall. You don't have to pay for booth rental fees or commissions. You don't have the travel expenses involved in selling at shows, nor the cost of acquiring displays. And a bonus is that you don't have to haul your inventory and booth displays all over the state or country.

Easier to scale: When you sell on Etsy, it's easy to scale your business up or down depending on your needs. You can list more items when you have a lot of inventory, or you can take a break when you need to focus on other things. There is no pressure to stock a booth or acquire inventory for a flea market. Instead, you can focus on sourcing the very best products and listing them when you have the time. The only thing that limits your ability to scale your business is having the space to store your inventory.

Etsy versus eBay: When it comes to selling antiques and vintage collectibles, it can be tempting to choose eBay and not consider Etsy. After all, eBay is the third largest online marketplace behind Amazon and Walmart. eBay has a huge customer base and a trusted reputation as the place for shoppers to find deals on everything from clothing and toys to collectibles and even cars.

However, while eBay certainly has its advantages, there are several reasons why Etsy may be the better choice for antique and vintage sellers specifically. First and foremost, Etsy has a dedicated customer base specifically looking for vintage items. Etsy shoppers come to the site to find hard-to-find items to add to their collections. This means that they are often willing to pay more for vintage and antique pieces, and they are more likely to appreciate the time and effort that goes into sourcing and presenting high-quality items for sale. In contrast, eBay shoppers are often looking for deals and may be less interested in the unique history of antique and vintage items, therefore not understanding their true value.

Another advantage of selling on Etsy is the ability to create a shop with a particular aesthetic. Etsy allows sellers to customize their storefronts with photos, descriptions, and branding that can help to create a unique identity. This is great for sellers who specialize in niche areas of vintage collecting, as it allows them to stand out from the competition and build a loyal following. If you specialize in ephemera, for example, you can build a shop that showcases the postcards, stationery, and cards you have for sale, making your store the go-to place for collectors.

Etsy shoppers also tend to look at a seller's shop, not just the item they searched for. On eBay, buyers usually search for a particular item and only look at the listings that show up for them in search. They look for the lowest price and buy that item, not bothering to look at the seller's other items.

However, Etsy shoppers are more likely to click through to a seller's shop and browse all of the products they have for sale. This leads to a higher likelihood of making a sale, including a customer buying multiple items from one shop in the same transaction. If they are happy with their purchase, they will also be more likely to become a repeat customer by favoring your shop and being notified of your new listings.

Etsy shoppers tend to have high expectations when it comes to customer service. They expect top-notch service, including prompt and professional communication, careful packaging, and quick shipping times. They also expect sellers to be knowledgeable about the antiques they are selling, including their history and specific condition. While this may cause sellers some stress, I personally look at it as an advantage over other sellers in the market. If you have a good understanding of vintage collectibles and antiques, particularly the ones you have for sale, you can gain shoppers' trust as you will be able to provide detailed and accurate information about the items you are selling

Etsy's Demographics: Although Etsy may not be as large as e-commerce giants like Amazon or eBay, the platform has experienced steady growth in recent years. As of 2022, Etsy has nearly 100 million active users, and generated $2.5 billion in revenue, representing a 10% increase from the previous year. With nearly 8 million sellers on the platform, there is a great balance between supply and demand, as the site also boasts nearly 94 million active buyers.

In the vintage category specifically, Etsy has surpassed $1.2 billion in gross merchandise sales since 2020. With an aging population that has disposable income to spend and a renewed interest in obtaining the collectibles they remember from their childhoods, there is no shortage of buyers ready and willing to shop on Etsy.

The choice is clear: With a website built for selling antiques and a customer base eager to buy vintage collectibles, the question isn't why would you sell on Etsy but why wouldn't you?

CHAPTER TWO: EQUIPMENT YOU NEED TO SELL ON ETSY

Are you new to selling online? Do you feel intimidated by technology? Have you convinced yourself that you don't have the computer skills to run an online business? If so, please don't worry! With just a few essential pieces of equipment and the most basic of computer skills, you can start selling antiques and vintage collectibles on Etsy.

In this chapter, we'll go over what exactly you'll need to open a successful Etsy shop, from a computer and internet access to a camera and shipping supplies. Even if you're not tech-savvy, we will break down all of the requirements into easy-to-understand terms, so you can confidently start your Etsy shop. Whether you plan to sell antiques as a hobby or as a full-time business, this chapter will help you gather everything you need on the back end.

Computer & Internet: To sell on Etsy, you need a computer with internet access. Note that some people run their Etsy shops completely on their smartphones, but the vast majority of sellers use desktop or laptop computers for most tasks. If you already have a computer system, you will likely be able to use what you already have to sell on Etsy. I use a Dell laptop but have also used HP and Apple computers to run my e-commerce businesses.

If you don't have a computer, here are some basic specifics to look for in a system that is ideal for selling on Etsy:

- Processor: At least an Intel Core i3 or AMD Ryzen 3 processor
- Memory (RAM): At least 8GB of RAM
- Storage: At least 256GB solid-state drive (SSD) or hard disk drive (HDD)

These specifics boil down to a computer with a fast processor (to make a listing on Etsy quick and easy) that has a decent amount of memory and storage (for saving photos and graphics). I always buy a computer with the fastest processor and the largest amount of memory and storage I can afford as I'd rather have too much power than not enough.

As for the internet, you want a stable and fast connection that will enable you to list products, ship orders, and handle customer questions in a timely manner. These days almost all internet companies promise fast and reliable access. I log on and off of Etsy several times a day to manage my shop, and a steady internet connection makes sure I don't miss a beat. I get internet from the same provider that manages my telephone and cable television.

Printer: Having a printer is essential for running an Etsy shop as you will need to print packing slips and shipping labels. The two most common types of printers used by Etsy sellers are LaserJet printers and thermal label printers.

LaserJet printers are the most commonly used types of printers for printing shipping labels and packing slips for new Etsy sellers as most people already have these types of printers in their homes. Note that Inkjet printers also serve the same function. You can print labels out onto paper that you then tape to shipping boxes or onto peel-and-stick label sheets. I am not ashamed to admit that for years I printed my shipping labels onto printer paper and then taped them to the shipping boxes! I eventually began using peel-and-stick label sheets, which print two labels per page.

The pros of using a LaserJet (or inkjet) printer are that they are more versatile and can handle a wider range of printing tasks than a dedicated label printer. You can print on different types of paper using various fonts and colors. A high-quality color printer can even print graphics and photos. And the basic models of these printers are less expensive than dedicated label printers.

The cons of using an LaserJet printer for an Etsy business are that they may not be as efficient as a dedicated label printer, as they require manual loading of label sheets and can be slower to print. However, this is only an issue if you are shipping out dozens of orders per day. Most vintage and antique sellers sell higher-priced items, not low-dollar items, meaning they usually have fewer orders to ship every day. The exception would be during the busy holiday shopping season.

Thermal label printers, in contrast, are specifically designed for printing labels and are often used by businesses that do a lot of shipping, including Etsy shops. These printers use heat to transfer ink onto the label and do not require ink cartridges or toner. Rollo is the most popular brand of thermal printer; I use one to print my Etsy shipping labels.

The pros of using a thermal label printer are that they are generally faster and more efficient than Inkjet or LaserJet printers when it comes to printing labels. They also produce high-quality, smudge-free labels that are easy to read. You simply print a label onto a label sheet, peel of the backing, and stick it to the pages.

The cons of using a thermal label printer are that they can be more expensive than LaserJet printers, and they may not be as versatile, as they are specifically designed for label printing and cannot be used for other printing tasks. While you don't need to buy ink for these printers, you do need to purchase special labels.

I have both a LaserJet printer and a thermal printer for my Etsy shop. I use the LaserJet to print packing slips and the thermal printer to print shipping labels.

Smartphone: When I first started selling online, I used a digital camera to take photos of my products. I then had to transfer the digital files to my computer and upload them to eBay. While it was tedious, it was still easier than in the old days when sellers had to use film cameras, develop the photos, and then scan them in!

Thankfully, technology has come a long way since then. Nowadays, smartphones, both Apple and Android, have cameras that take better photos than most traditional cameras. I use my iPhone to take all of my product photos. I can even edit the photos directly on my phone before uploading them to my Etsy listings through the Etsy app.

Beyond taking listing photos, having a smartphone with the Etsy app downloaded onto it allows you to manage your business on the go. This includes answering customer messages promptly, which is crucial in meeting Etsy's high expectations of providing excellent customer service. I have notifications enabled on my iPhone so that I am alerted when a new order or message comes in.

Photography Area: A smartphone is essential for taking and uploading photos to Etsy, but you also need a place to take those photos. Having a dedicated space to take pictures of the antiques you are selling is an important part of a successful online business as one of the most important aspects of selling antiques on Etsy is having great photos of your products. Your photographs need to be clear, and crisp, and showcase the unique features of each item you are selling. In a sea of similar Etsy listings, great pictures will help you stand out from the competition.

You don't need to have a professional photography studio set up to take great Etsy photos, however. You do need a designated photography area in your home or workspace. I have a corner in my office that is set up with white posterboard backdrops. The table is next to a window for some natural light during the day, but I mainly rely on lamps to provide lighting so that I can take photos at any time.

Good lighting is essential to capturing the details and colors of your antiques. If you are short on natural light and aren't getting very good light from lamps, you may consider purchasing a tabletop lightbox. These can be found on Amazon for under $30. Lightboxes comes in various sizes; you want to make sure the size you choose can accommodate the types of items you sell. If you mainly sell jewelry, a small lightbox will suffice. However, you sell large figurines, you will want a bigger model.

In addition to lighting, you also need to have a good backdrop for your photos. A white or neutral-colored backdrop is ideal for photographing antiques. I use white foam boards that I buy at Dollar Tree for my backdrops. White works best for most items, although I also have black foam boards on hand for photographing light-colored glass.

Regardless of what you use for your backdrops, the main thing you need to ensure quality pictures is that the focus is on the item being sold, rather than the background. While some sellers like to add props to their listing pictures, I don't recommend this as some customers might assume that they are buying everything pictured, not only the item you are actually selling.

Etsy allows you to add 10 photos to each listing, and I encourage you to use all 10 slots. Take photos of your item from every angle, including from the top down and the bottom. You want shoppers to have the same view as if they were holding the piece and turning it over in their hands.

Inventory Storage: One of the biggest challenges for online sellers, particularly those selling antiques, is finding adequate storage space for their inventory. Antiques, often referred to as "hard goods" by resellers, require considerably more storage space than other types of inventory, such as clothing. To ensure the safety and protection of your products, it's essential to implement a proper storage solution that guards against damage, dirt, and moisture, while also allowing for easy access when orders come in.

Vintage items are often fragile and require special care when stored. If you're already selling your items in an antique mall or shop, you're likely familiar with how easy it is to damage collectibles. However, selling online eliminates the worry of customers damaging your items while browsing in person. But even with this advantage, without proper storage, your antiques can suffer from scratches, chips, or breakage.

As a seller of antiques and vintage collectibles, I've had my share of damage from items falling off shelves or getting scratched while attempting to cram more inventory into limited space. To prevent this, I use industrial shelving and totes for smaller items. Despite efficient storage methods, I still find myself rearranging inventory and investing in new shelving as my business grows. A 700-square-foot section of my basement is dedicated to inventory storage, but it never seems to be enough.

However, a large storage space isn't necessary for successful inventory storage. Many sellers utilize plastic storage tubs to store their inventory. While this method enables the storage of more items and protects them from dust, it requires an inventory management system to keep track of the products in each tote. If you're short on space, this method can work wonders. I know Etsy sellers who store over one thousand items in storage totes in their spare bedrooms!

PRO TIP: An "inventory management system" isn't as complicated as it sounds. In fact, Etsy makes the process easy by offering sellers a *Stock Keeping Unit*, or SKU, a field in all listings.

An SKU is a unique identifier code used to keep track of individual items in your inventory. When you create a new listing on Etsy, you have the option to add an SKU to that item. By adding an SKU to your Etsy inventory, you can easily track your inventory levels and ensure that your listings accurately reflect your available stock. You simply types in the SKU into the Etsy listing and then write that same number onto a sticker that you attach to your item.

Using the same SKU system for the storage totes or shelves you use to store inventory also helps keep you organized. For example, if you have SKU's numbered 001-025 that all fit in the same tote or on the same shelf, you can label that tote or shelf SKU001-025. Then when item SKU013 sells, you can go straight to SKU001-025 to find it.

Shipping Supplies: While inventory takes up the most room when running an Etsy shop, in second place are all of the supplies you need to ship out orders. Just as you have a dedicated space for taking photos, you will need a designated area for shipping. For reference, my shipping area consists of two folding banquet tables that hold boxes, bubble wrap, and packing paper. I have a shelving unit where I store other boxes. And I put totes of more shipping supplies under the tables. As for where I do my shipping? That's on a separate table!

The size of shipping boxes and the amount of packing materials you need to keep on hand will depend on the items you sell. If you only sell vintage jewelry, you will only need small jewelry boxes and bubble mailers to ship orders in. If you sell vintage clothing, you will only need poly mailers. However, if, like me, you sell a wide variety of antiques, you will need a wide variety of different sized shipping boxes on hand.

We'll discuss shipping in more detail later on in this book, but for now, here's an overview of the shipping supplies you will want to have on hand to sell on Etsy:

Digital Postage Scale: The first item you want to add to your shipping area is a digital postal scale to weigh packages to figure out the correct postage. You can buy digital scales for around $20 to $30 on Amazon, and they are also sold at office supply stores. Look for a "postage/mail" specific scale that measures pounds AND ounces, as you will need to know ounces when shipping items under one pound.

USPS Priority Mail boxes: The United States Postal Service, or USPS, offers free Priority Mail shipping boxes in various sizes that you can order online or pick up at your local post office. These boxes are specifically designed for shipping through the USPS Priority Mail service, which offers fast and affordable shipping with tracking and insurance included. We'll discuss these boxes further later on in this book, but for now, just understand that you will likely be utilizing these for your Etsy business.

Cardboard shipping boxes: While it's preferable to use the free USPS Priority Mail boxes, the fact is that not all products will fit into the limited sizes the Post Office carries. Therefore, you will want to keep a wide variety of plain cardboard shipping boxes on hand. I keep every sturdy, clean box that I get my own personal deliveries in. And I invest in shipping boxes that I buy on Amazon.

Bubble wrap: If you sell hard goods, then bubble wrap is a must. Bubble wrap protects items during shipping and is essential when shipping delicate antiques. I buy my bubble wrap from warehouse clubs such as Sam's Club and Costco as well as on Amazon. I also save any good, clean bubble wrap that I get in my own online orders.

Packing peanuts: Packing peanuts are those sticky little bits of Styrofoam that people often curse at when opening up a package, but if you sell glass or other delicate items, it is a must to add to your shipping area. I buy packing peanuts in bulk from Amazon and keep them in a container that was, no joke, marketed to hold dog food! I use a cat litter box scoop (again, no joke!) to scoop out the peanuts as the slots prevent static from building.

Packing paper: Having plain packing paper on hand is essential for adding padding to your shipping boxes. I buy plain newspaper rolls on Amazon. This paper is strong yet can easily be crumpled to tuck into corners of shipping boxes and to wrap around items.

Tissue paper: Tissue paper is perfect for wrapping up delicate items such as jewelry and miniatures. I also use it to tuck around fragile figurines before adding a layer of bubble wrap. Around the holidays, most warehouse clubs stock large rolls of tissue paper at a great price. After the holidays, you can usually find packages of tissue paper on clearance. I also buy packages of unused tissue paper at estate sales.

Shipping tape: Shipping tape, not packing tape, is another essential addition to your shipping station. I buy mine in bulk from the warehouse clubs, stocking up whenever they have a special offer. I also have several tape dispensers that I use, both handheld and the heavy tabletop variety.

Shipping labels: The printer you use will determine the shipping labels you will need. I use both a thermal printer and a LaserJet printer, so I have both thermal shipping labels and letter-size sheets of peel-and-stick labels that print two to a page.

Enclosures: Some sellers like to include enclosures in their packages. Over the years I've included business cards, postcards, stickers, and magnets in my packages, all of which I created to not only thank customers but to make sure they had my Etsy shop URL. I use Vistaprint for business cards and postcards and Sticker Mule for stickers and magnets.

PRO TIP: If you are new to selling online, then this chapter may have overwhelmed you. There are a lot of things you need to run a successful

Etsy shop, with inventory being only one piece of it. However, as you slowly work to build your inventory, you can slowly grow your storage and shipping supplies. Start by listing small items that can fit in the free USPS Priority Mail boxes and that only need bubble wrap and shipping tape. As you become more comfortable selling, you can add to your collection of supplies. Rome wasn't built in a day, and neither was any reseller's office!

CHAPTER THREE: WHAT TYPES OF ANTIQUES SELL BEST ON ETSY

Whether you are just starting out selling antiques or have a long history of selling vintage collectibles, you may be wondering which types of products sell best on Etsy. I've sold a wide variety secondhand items on Etsy, including glassware, ceramics, China dishes, silverware, toys, books, ephemera, and more. The list of what you can sell on Etsy is seemingly endless, but there is another list you need to educate yourself on: What items you *cannot* sell on Etsy.

As we've previously discussed, Etsy has three main categories: *Handmade, Craft Supplies*, and *Vintage*. But under each of these three main category are dozens of subcategories and niches. Etsy defines anything at least 20 years old as *Vintage*. However, just because an item meets the age requirement doesn't necessarily mean you can sell it on Etsy. It's important to review Etsy's prohibited items list to ensure that the antiques you plan to sell comply with Etsy's policies.

Here is a list of items that Etsy excludes from being sold on its website:

1. Alcohol
2. Drugs and drug paraphernalia
3. Tobacco and tobacco products
4. Fireworks and explosives
5. Firearms and weapons
6. Human remains or body parts
7. Hazardous materials
8. Live animals
9. Pornography and adult content
10. Stolen property or items that promote or glorify violence or hate groups

11. Items that violate intellectual property rights
12. Recalled items
13. Personal information or mailing lists

Antique sellers in particular need to be aware of a few of these prohibited items on Etsy. For instance, while you cannot sell alcohol on Etsy, you can sell ephemera and collectibles from alcohol brands. The same applies to tobacco products; you cannot sell tobacco itself, but you can sell vintage pipes and cigarette cases.

Another category to be mindful of when listing antiques is hazardous materials. If you plan to sell old bottles or containers, make sure they are empty and, if possible, have been thoroughly cleaned. It's important to avoid listing items that contain hazardous substances or pose a risk to the health and safety of the buyer or anyone handling the package during shipping.

When selling antiques on Etsy, you need to be aware of the rules surrounding licensed products, particularly those with well-known brands or characters like Disney collectibles. While you can sell vintage branded items that feature licensed characters or logos, such as an antique Mickey Mouse toy, you cannot sell reproductions of these licensed products on Etsy.

Reproductions are items that are made to look like the original item but are not authentic, such as a fake Mickey Mouse watch or a copy of a vintage Disney poster. Selling reproductions of licensed products can lead to copyright infringement and legal issues for both the seller and Etsy. It's important to only sell authentic vintage items and avoid listing any reproductions that could potentially infringe on someone else's intellectual property rights. And even licensed products that are made to look vintage, such as Disney licensed reproductions, cannot be listed on Etsy unless that are at least 20 years old.

Finally, you must research every item you plan to sell to see if it has been recalled. A recall is when a product is deemed unsafe for consumers and is removed from the market. In the United States, the Consumer Product Safety Commission (CPSC) is responsible for enforcing product safety standards and issuing recalls when necessary.

To check if an item has been recalled, you can start by searching the CPSC's recall database. This database allows you to search for recalls by product type, brand name, or keyword. It's important to check this database regularly, as new recalls are added frequently.

In addition to the CPSC database, it's a good idea to check other sources for potential recalls. For example, if you plan to sell vintage toys, you may want to check the Toy Industry Association's recall database. If you plan to sell antique furniture, you may want to check for any recalls related to furniture safety.

An instance of a vintage toy that was recalled that you cannot resell on Etsy or anywhere online is the Cabbage Patch Kids Snacktime Kid Doll. In 1996, this toy was recalled due to safety concerns. The doll had a motorized mouth that would "eat" plastic snacks, but some children were getting their fingers or hair caught in the mechanism, leading to injuries. Therefore, you cannot sell this doll online, even if the person buying it just wants it for display with no intention to play with it.

Now that you know what you cannot sell on Etsy, let's turn our attention to what you can sell on the platform. Most antiques and vintage collectibles will sell well on Etsy, including:

Mid-century modern: Mid-century modern (MCM for short) furniture and decor pieces from the 1950s and 1960s are highly sought after by Etsy shoppers who collect this aesthetic. This style is characterized by clean lines, bold colors, and a sleek, minimalist aesthetic.

When you sell antiques, learning about brands, patterns, and other details never ends. If you are unfamiliar with mid-century modern vintage items, you'll want to spend time searching Etsy to see what other sellers are offering. Here are some popular brands that you will want to learn about:

1. **Coro:** Coro was a popular mid-century costume jewelry brand known for its whimsical and playful designs. Look for pieces with colorful rhinestones or enamel accents.

2. **McCoy:** McCoy is a mid-century pottery brand known for its colorful and unique designs. Look for pieces like planters, vases, and pitchers.

3. **Napco:** Napco is a vintage figurine brand known for its adorable ceramic figurines, including animals, angels, and other decorative items.

4. **Pyrex:** Pyrex is a mid-century glassware brand known for its bright colors and bold patterns. Look for pieces like mixing bowls, baking dishes, and serving bowls.

5. **Russell Wright:** Russell Wright is a mid-century modernist known for his designs in dinnerware, furniture, and other decorative items. Look for pieces like serving dishes, pitchers, and dinnerware.

6. **Stangl:** Stangl is a mid-century pottery brand known for its unique designs and bright colors. Look for pieces like vases, planters, and dinnerware.

When sourcing mid-century modern pieces, it is important to pay attention to dates and markings. Mid-century modern pieces are typically dated from the 1950s through the 1960s. Look for pieces that have a clear date stamp or marking, as this can increase their value. Additionally, some mid-century modern pieces were manufactured in specific countries, such as Japan or the United States, which can also impact their value.

The most popular mid-century modern pieces are typically brightly colored and have bold patterns with unique shapes. Blue, gold, pink, and mint green are all popular among collectors. Note that the avocado green and burnt orange that were in many homes in the 60s aren't as popular as they were so common. I have yet to go to an estate sale that doesn't have at least one piece of brown kitchenware, which I never pick up to resell.

Pattens also play a big part in the ability to command top dollar for mid-century modern collectibles, including:

1. **Atomic:** The atomic pattern is characterized by abstract, atomic-like shapes and often incorporates bright, bold colors.
2. **Boomerang:** The boomerang pattern features curved, boomerang-like shapes and is often seen in textiles like pillows and upholstery.
3. **Dots:** Mid-century modern designs often incorporate simple, graphic dot patterns in bright colors.
4. **Geometric:** Mid-century modern designs often feature bold, graphic geometric patterns in a variety of shapes and colors.
5. **Mod Floral:** Mid-century modern floral patterns often feature bold, graphic designs in bright colors, with a stylized, abstract feel.
6. **Starburst:** The starburst pattern features a burst of lines radiating from a central point, often seen in wall clocks, mirrors, and other decorative items.

If you're new to selling on Etsy, it's best to start with smaller mid-century modern items that are easier to ship, including:

1. **Barware:** Mid-century modern barware, including cocktail shakers, glasses, and decanters, can be easy to find and ship. These items are typically smaller and lighter than furniture or

lamps and can be shipped using standard shipping methods.

2. **Desk accessories:** Mid-century modern desk accessories, such as pen holders, desk lamps, and paperweights, can be easy to photograph, list, and ship. These items are typically small and light and can be shipped using standard shipping methods.

3. **Kitchenware:** Mid-century modern kitchenware, including mixing bowls, serving dishes, and utensils, can be easy to find and ship. These items are typically smaller and lighter than furniture or lamps and can be shipped using standard shipping methods.

4. **Small home decor items:** Mid-century modern home decor items, such as vases, figurines, and bookends, can be easy to find and ship. These items are typically smaller and lighter than furniture or lamps and can be shipped using standard shipping methods.

5. **Wall decor:** Mid-century modern wall decor, such as mirrors, art prints, and wall clocks, can be easy to photograph, list, and ship. These items are typically flat and lightweight and can be shipped using standard shipping methods.

When it comes to larger mid-century modern furniture pieces, such as sofas, dressers, or dining tables, note that unless your customer is local that it will necessary to arrange for freight shipping. Freight shipping involves using a shipping carrier that specializes in large and heavy items, and it is much more complicated and costly than standard shipping methods. To arrange for freight shipping, you'll need to find a reputable carrier that specializes in furniture shipping. This will involve obtaining quotes from multiple carriers to find the best rates and options. And it's important to properly package and prepare the furniture for shipping to ensure it arrives at its destination in good condition.

If you're not comfortable with arranging freight shipping but you have MCM furniture, consider selling your larger mid-century modern furniture pieces locally or through a consignment shop. This will help you avoid the complications and expenses associated with freight shipping while still reaching a local market of buyers who are interested in mid-century modern furniture. Since vintage furniture is plentiful but often overlooked at garage sales, flipping these pieces locally via Facebook Marketplace can be profitable while you save your smaller pieces for Etsy.

Vintage clothing and accessories: Vintage clothing and accessories from the 1920s through the 1980s are popular on Etsy. This includes dresses, coats, hats, and handbags. Just like with hard goods, to be considered vintage, clothing and accessories must be at least 20 years old.

When selling vintage clothing and accessories, be sure to accurately describe the condition of each item. Buyers expect vintage items to show small signs of wear and tear, but they still want items that are in good overall condition. It's not uncommon to find significant stains or rips on vintage clothing, so if you are not willing to repair these flaws, avoid picking up such pieces.

While vintage clothing with flaws can still sell, if you do list flawed items, be sure to take clear photos of all the item's issues. Unlike modern clothing sellers who typically wash secondhand items before listing them for sale, vintage clothing is often too fragile to withstand a washing machine cycle. Instead, many vintage clothing sellers prefer to steam their items. For small stains, you may be able to spot-treat them using a Tide pen or Shout wipe.

Vintage clothing and accessories come in a wide range of styles, from classic 1950s dresses to 1980s neon punk rock jackets. Pay attention to current fashion trends and what's popular among vintage enthusiasts to help you identify the most in-demand styles. You can also find active vintage clothing communities on social media platforms such as Instagram, TikTok, and Pinterest.

As for brands, there are hundreds of popular vintage labels you'll want to look for to sell on Etsy, including:

Adidas: Adidas is a sportswear brand that has been around since the 1940s. Vintage Adidas clothing and accessories, particularly from the 1980s and 1990s, are popular among collectors. The Adidas trefoil logo was introduced in 1972, so vintage Adidas items made before that time will not have the logo. However, after 1997, Adidas introduced a new logo that replaced the trefoil. So look for vintage Adidas items with the trefoil logo to help identify their age.

Look for vintage Adidas pieces that are representative of a particular era or style, such as the bold colors and patterns of the 1980s and 1990s. Popular vintage Adidas items to sell on Etsy include track jackets, sneakers, and t-shirts. Other popular vintage sportswear brands to look for include Nike, Reebok, and Puma.

Chanel: Chanel is a luxury fashion brand known for its timeless designs featuring their iconic CC logo. Vintage Chanel clothing and accessories are highly coveted by fashionistas and collectors alike. Because Chanel is so valuable, there are many counterfeit Chanel items on the market. When sourcing vintage Chanel items, it's important to look for authenticity markers like the hologram sticker on the inside of a handbag or the authenticity card that accompanies some Chanel jewelry pieces.

Chanel has been around since the early 1900s, and the brand's designs have evolved. Look for vintage Chanel pieces that are representative of a particular era or style, such as the classic quilted handbags that were introduced in the 1950s or the bold, oversized jewelry of the 1980s. Popular vintage Chanel items to sell on Etsy include handbags, jewelry, clothing, and accessories like scarves and sunglasses. Classic designs like the Chanel 2.55 handbag, the Chanel No. 5 perfume, and the iconic interlocking CC logo are all highly sought after by collectors.

Dior: Dior is a luxury fashion brand known for its elegant, feminine designs. Vintage Dior clothing and accessories are highly collectible, with shoppers scouring Etsy, eBay, and Poshmark for pieces to add to their collections. Like Chanel, Dior is a brand that is often counterfeited. When sourcing vintage Dior items, look for authenticity markers like the "CD" logo on jewelry pieces or the "Christian Dior" label on clothing and handbags.

Dior has been around since the late 1940s, and the brand's designs have evolved. Look for vintage Dior pieces that are representative of a particular era or style, such as the *New Look* designs of the 1950s or the bold, colorful patterns of the 1970s. Popular vintage Dior items to sell on Etsy include clothing, handbags, and jewelry. Classic designs like the Lady Dior handbag and the Diorissimo perfume are also highly collectible.

Levi's: Levi's is a classic American denim brand that has been around since the 1800s. Vintage Levi's denim jeans and jackets are highly sought after by collectors, especially overseas. Vintage Levi's jeans will have a red tab on the back pocket that features the Levi's logo. This red tab was first introduced in 1936 and has been a signature feature of Levi's jeans ever since.

On vintage Levi's jeans, the tag on the back of the waistband will have a capital "E" on it, rather than a lowercase "e". This "E" indicates that the jeans were made before 1971. You also want to Look for selvage denim, which is woven on old-fashioned shuttle looms and has a self-finished edge. Vintage Levi's jeans made before the 1980s often feature selvage denim.

Pendleton: Pendleton is an American woolen mill that has been producing high-quality wool products since the 1800s. Vintage Pendleton wool shirts, jackets, and blankets are popular. Pendleton items will have a label that can help you identify their age. Vintage Pendleton labels will feature the words *Pendleton Woolen Mills* or *Pendleton's* along with a small, circular logo. has been around since the early 1900s.

Look for vintage Pendleton pieces that are representative of a particular era or style, such as the colorful, geometric patterns of the 1960s or the more subdued, earthy tones of the 1970s. Popular vintage Pendleton items to sell on Etsy include wool blankets, jackets, and shirts. Classic designs like the Pendleton *Chief Joseph* blanket and the Pendleton *49er* jacket are highly sought after.

Wrangler: Wrangler is another classic American denim brand that has been around since the 1940s. Vintage Wrangler denim pieces are popular among collectors, many of whom are based overseas. Like Levi's, vintage Wrangler jeans will have a tag on the back of the waistband that can help you identify their age. Vintage Wrangler jeans made before the mid-1970s will have a single, capital letter on the tag, while those made after the mid-1970s will have a mix of letters and numbers.

Vintage Wrangler jeans often have unique features that make them desirable to collectors. For example, the Wrangler 11MWZ jeans, which were introduced in 1947, have a distinctive "W" stitching on the back pockets that can help you identify them as vintage. Popular vintage Wrangler items to sell on Etsy include denim jackets, jeans, and shirts. The Wrangler 11MWZ jeans and the Wrangler denim jacket are also highly sought after.

Handmade clothing: Handmade vintage clothing is becoming increasingly popular among collectors on Etsy. Here are some things to look for when sourcing handmade vintage clothing:

Handmade vintage clothing can be especially unique and well-made, but the quality of craftsmanship can vary greatly. Look for pieces that have clean stitching and finishes, as well as unique design features that make them stand out.

Handmade vintage clothing often features unique or rare fabrics that may be harder to find today. Look for pieces that feature fabrics like silk, lace, or vintage prints that are characteristic of a particular era or style. Some handmade vintage clothing styles are more popular than others. For example, women's dresses from the 1950s and 1960s, men's suits from the 1940s and 1950s, and baby clothes from the 1920s and 1930s are all popular among vintage clothing collectors.

In addition to clothing, vintage accessories such as purses and hats are also popular items on Etsy. Selling vintage accessories can be a great way to diversify your Etsy shop and appeal to a wider range of customers. Plus, accessories are usually easier to handle versus clothing because they are smaller, meaning they are easier to photograph, list, store, and ship.

Look for pieces that have held up well over time and show minimal signs of wear and tear. Some vintage accessory brands and designers are more desirable than others. Research popular vintage accessory brands like Gucci, Hermès, and Louis Vuitton, as well as smaller boutique brands that may have a dedicated following. Some vintage accessory styles are more popular than others. For example, vintage leather purses from the 1960s and 1970s, silk scarves from the 1950s and 1960s, and vintage hats from the 1920s and 1930s are all popular among vintage accessory collectors.

Vintage jewelry: Vintage jewelry, including costume and fine jewelry, is a popular category on Etsy. Jewelry is a great niche to sell in because it is small, making it easy to list, store, and ship. Broaches, rings, clip-on earrings, and large statement pieces made from coloring stones are always popular with shoppers.

While sterling silver (mark 925) and solid gold jewelry featuring diamonds, emeralds, and rubies are obviously going to fetch a high price regardless of where they are sold, vintage costume jewelry is much more accessible at estate sales, garage sales, and thrift stores, meaning you will have better luck finding pieces there to resell on Etsy. Some popular vintage costume jewelry brands include:

- Coro
- Hobe
- Juliana
- Kramer
- Lisner
- Monet
- Napier
- Sarah Coventry
- Trifari
- Weiss

Aside from precious metals and jewels, Enamel, Bakelite, and Lucite are popular materials to look for in vintage jewelry pieces. Enamel jewelry is made by fusing glass with metal, creating a smooth, glossy surface. Bakelite is a type of plastic that was popular in the mid-20th century. And Lucite, a type of plastic that was popular in the 1940s and 1950s, is clear. If you plan to sell vintage jewelry, learning how to identify these three materials will help you spot the best pieces and make more money.

When sourcing for vintage jewelry to sell on Etsy, be sure to check for the maker's mark engraved on the back of the piece. This mark can provide valuable information about the piece's origin, age, and authenticity. Carrying a jeweler's loop, which is a small magnifier, with you can help you quickly identify any marks on the jewelry you find.

In addition to checking for the maker's mark, be sure to inspect the quality and condition of the piece. Look for vintage jewelry that is made from high-quality materials like gold, silver, or platinum, and that features unique and interesting designs. Consider the overall condition of the piece as well, looking for minimal signs of damage or wear and tear. Broken clasps or missing stones can seriously devalue a piece.

When listing vintage jewelry on Etsy, take clear, high-quality photos of each piece and provide detailed descriptions that accurately describe the item's condition, size, and unique features. Investing in a ring sizer, jewelry display stands, and books about vintage jewelry will not only help you source the best products but will help you perfect your listings.

In addition to design and materials, vintage jewelry sets are also very popular among buyers. Look for complete sets, such as necklaces with matching earrings or bracelets, to increase their value and desirability. If the sets are in their original boxes, they will bring in even more money.

Vintage cameras and photography equipment: Vintage cameras and photography equipment from the 20th century can be a lucrative niche on Etsy. This includes film cameras, lenses, and other accessories. Undeveloped film is particularly valuable, as are unused flash bulbs.

Vintage toys: Vintage toys are a popular category of antiques and collectibles that can be sold on Etsy. From classic board games to action figures and dolls, vintage toys hold a special place in the hearts of collectors, which means they will pay up for the chance to reclaim a piece of their childhood. Whether you are an experienced antique seller or just starting out, selling vintage toys on Etsy is not only profitable but also a lot of fun!

Here are some of the best vintage toy categories for making money on Etsy:

Action figures: Vintage action figures from the 1970s and 1980s, such as Star Wars, G.I. Joe, and He-Man, are highly sought after by collectors. Condition is crucial when it comes to getting top dollar for action figures. While some people purchase damaged figures for replacement parts, most Etsy shoppers are looking for figures that are in excellent condition with their original clothing.

Action figures typically have the maker's mark etched on them. However, be aware of remakes, as many vintage dolls have been redesigned and re-released by the original makers. For instance, you can find new reproduction Star Wars figures at Walmart and Target. If you plan to sell action figures, you need to educate yourself on how to distinguish between the vintage versions and the modern ones.

Board games: Classic board games from the 1950s, 1960s, and 1970s are popular vintage toys and can include early releases of titles such as Monopoly, Clue, and Risk. The trick with board games is to make sure they are complete and don't have missing pieces. The box needs to be in excellent condition, too. The downside to selling games is that they are often an odd shape that requires a specialty-sized shipping box, which also means they cost more to ship.

Cars and trucks: Vintage toy cars and trucks are popular with collectors, particularly those from the 1950s and 1960s. Etsy sellers look for brands such as Matchbox, Hot Wheels, and Tonka, nothing the condition as damaged or missing parts will negatively affect the asking price.

Sellers of vintage cars and trucks have learned how to spot older toys from new releases. For example, some vintage Hot Wheels cars have red lines on the tires, which were a distinctive feature in the 1960s and early 1970s.

Another way to identify vintage toy cars is by looking at the packaging to see if you can spot the date of manufacture or the country in which the toy was made. Toys made in Japan, the United States, Korea, West Germany, and Taiwan are almost always vintage. If the package reads "Made In China," it is likely a new release.

Dolls: Vintage dolls, particularly those from the 1950s and 1960s, can be highly collectible. Look for popular brands such as Barbie, Madame Alexander, Roche, and Betsy McCall. Ensure that the dolls have all of their hair intact, as children often give their dolls haircuts. Also, check the fingers of the dolls, as many vintage dolls may have lost a digit or two over the years. You can usually find the doll maker's mark on the back of the doll's head or printed on the back.

Tin toys: Vintage tin toys, such as wind-up cars and robots, can be highly sought after by collectors. Look for brands such as Marx and Lehmann. Tin toys were often made in Japan in the mid-20th century and feature bright colors, and intricate designs, and often include wind-up mechanisms. Some of the most popular types of tin toys include robots, space toys, and vehicles such as cars and airplanes.

When looking for vintage tin toys to sell on Etsy, make sure to check for any damage or rust, as well as ensure that any wind-up mechanisms still work properly. If a wind-up toy no longer works but it still in good condition, you may still be able to sell it for part. As with other vintage toys, there are reproduction tin toys now being manufactured. Be sure to check for a date and county of manufacture (Japan and USA) on any tin toys you are thinking of listing on Etsy to be sure they are in fact vintage. Toys marked at *Made In China* are not vintage.

Disney Memorabilia: Vintage Disney memorabilia, including items such as plush toys and figurines, can be highly collectible. As with other vintage items sold on Etsy, Disney memorabilia must be at least 20 years old to be sold on the site. Fortunately, most vintage Disney items are stamped with a date and/or the country of manufacture. Look for items made in Japan, the United States, West Germany, Taiwan, and Korea to sell on Etsy, and avoid products marked *Made In China* unless they are stamped with a date that confirms they are vintage.

Many vintage Disney toys and merchandise will have the words *Walt Disney Productions* or *Walt Disney Company* on them, which can help indicate when the item was produced. Additionally, some vintage Disney items may have unique features or designs that are no longer used, such as the original Mickey Mouse design from the 1930s or the early "D" Disneyland logo. It's also important to note that there are many Disney reproductions and fakes on the market, so it's important to do your research to ensure the items you list are in fact vintage.

While most of the Disney items made feature Mickey Mouse or Minnie Mouse, it's the secondary Disney characters that are typically more valuable on sites like Etsy. For example, while you can find Mickey Mouse products in almost every store, Donald Duck items are harder to find, which makes them more valuable. I sell a lot of Disney vintage, and I am always looking for what is referred to as the *secondary characters*, those characters that haven't had as much merchandise made of their likeness.

Here are some popular categories of vintage Disney, also referred to as *Disneyana*, on Etsy:

1. **Books:** First editions of Disney books and rare editions, such as those from the Little Golden Books series, can be valuable to collectors.
2. **Ceramics:** This can include figurines, vases, and other decorative items.
3. **Clothing:** This can include t-shirts, sweatshirts, and even costumes from Disneyland and Disney World parks.
4. **Pins:** Disney has been producing pins since the 1980s, and vintage pins from past events and limited editions can be highly sought after.
5. **Posters:** Original Disney park posters from the 1950s and 1960s are highly sought after by collectors.
6. **Theme park memorabilia:** Park maps, brochures, postcards, and ephemera from Disneyland, Walt Disney World, and the international Disney parks are always in demand on Etsy.
7. **Toys:** Disney has been producing toys since the 1930s, and vintage toys like plushies and action figures can be highly collectible.
8. **Watches:** Disney has partnered with watchmakers over the years to release character and limited-edition watches.

Vintage kitchenware and dishware: Vintage kitchenware and dishware from the 1920s through the 1970s is a hot-selling category on Etsy. This includes Pyrex, Fire King, and other vintage brands. The upside of selling vintage kitchenware is that it is plentiful at garage sales, estate sales, and thrift stores. The downside is that many sellers know these pieces have value and tend to price them high, making it difficult to flip them for profit online.

Another issue with vintage dishware is condition. If the pieces were heavily used by the original owner, they may have cracks, chips, and scratches, which will lessen their value. These pieces are also usually heavy, meaning they cost more to ship. And because they are breakable, you will have to invest in packing supplies such as bubble wrap and packing peanuts, which will eat into your profits.

That's not to say you should consider selling these pieces. I always have my eye out for the following pieces, which I will pick up if they are in good condition and priced low:

1. Cookie jars
2. Depression-era glassware
3. Enamelware
4. Hand-blown glass vases
5. Hand-painted pottery and stoneware
6. Jadeite dishes
7. Large sets of silverware
8. Metal canisters and breadboxes
9. Mid-century modern barware
10. Pyrex and Fire King glassware
11. Recipe card boxes
12. Retro linens and tablecloths
13. Salt and pepper shakers
14. Tea sets and coffee pots
15. Tupperware

Vintage home décor: Home décor includes everything from figurines and holiday decorations to artwork and table lamps. These items can be made from a variety of materials, including ceramics, glass, and metal. The popularity of different styles and materials changes over time, but mid-century modern and kitschy styles are always in demand. When shopping for vintage home decor to sell on Etsy, it's look for unique and eye-catching pieces that will stand out in a home. And, of course, always be sure that items are free from damage such as cracks, chips, and faded paint.

Figurines: If you are new to selling antiques, figures are a great place to start as they can be found at garage sales, estate sales, and thrift stores at usually low prices. As always, condition counts, and the older a figurine is, the more valuable it will be. Also note that not all figures have resale value. When I am sourcing vintage figurines to resell, I look for the following brands:

1. Belleek
2. Fenton
3. Fitz and Floyd
4. Fontanini
5. Hummel/Goebel
6. Josef Originals
7. Lefton
8. Lladro
9. Noritake
10. Royal Doulton

I also look for figurines stamped as being made in Japan, the United States, or West Germany.

PRO TIP: Just as there are many valuable vintage figurines, there are just as many that have little to no value on Etsy. Precious Moments (except the Disney ones), Cherished Teddies, and Boyd's Bears fill the shelves at thrift stores for a reason: they just aren't worth much on the resale market. Learning what figurines aren't worth picking up is just as important as learning which are.

Vintage Holiday Décor: Vintage holiday decor and collectibles are a popular category on Etsy, and it's my favorite category to sell in. Christmas and Halloween are the most popular holiday items, but there is also a market for vintage Valentine's Day, Easter, and the 4th of July. Some popular vintage holiday items that sell well on Etsy include:

1. **Christmas ornaments:** Glass ornaments from the 1940s and 1950s are particularly popular, as are ornaments featuring iconic characters like Santa Claus and Rudolph the Red-Nosed Reindeer. Hallmark ornaments that feature light and motion, as well as some of the ornaments for certain series, can fetch a high price.
2. **Decorations:** Vintage decorations like tinsel trees, plastic blow mold figures, and ceramic figurines sell well year round.
3. **Linens:** Vintage tablecloths, napkins, and handkerchiefs featuring holiday themes like holly and mistletoe are popular with collectors.
4. **Music:** Vintage Christmas records, CDs, and sheet music are popular among collectors who not only listen to the music but also display the packaging.
5. **Cards and postcards:** Collectors love to add vintage holiday cards and postcards to their collections, particularly those featuring vintage artwork or iconic holiday images.

These are just some of the vintage items that sell well on Etsy. Take time to browse Etsy to see what other sellers have in their stores and what items are selling for to help you know what to pick up for your own shop.

CHAPTER FOUR: WHERE TO SOURCE ANTIQUES FOR RESALE

In the previous chapter, we covered just some of the vintage items you can sell on Etsy. But to sell an item, you first need to buy it. This is referred to as **sourcing** in the reselling community. The older term was **picking**, and **resellers** were referred to as **pickers**. But today *reselling, reseller,* and *sourcing* are the terms most people use. I personally prefer the term *reseller* to *picker*!

As we have already discussed, while many people refer to old items as antiques, most of what people are selling on Etsy is vintage. Antiques are technically 100 years old, while Etsy defines vintage as being at least 20 years old.

Regardless of what terms people use, the fact is that vintage collectibles are sold on the secondhand market at garage sales, estate sales, and thrift stores at a fraction of the cost of what they can fetch online. These are some of the best places to find vintage items to resell on Etsy. Not only can you score amazing deals, but you also have the thrill of the hunt. Most resellers say that sourcing is their favorite part of the job!

However, it can be overwhelming to know where to start when it comes to sourcing vintage items in bulk for an Etsy shop. If you've been slowly stocking an antique mall booth, you may have had years to find enough inventory to fill it. And sales likely come in at a trickle. Many antique dealers have more inventory than their shelves will hold.

However, when you transition to online selling, items typically sell much faster than in a brick-and-mortar store, meaning you will need to be sourcing more. After all, you are reselling to make money, and you can't make money if you don't have inventory for sale. If you already have inventory, list those items first before you source more.

If you are new to reselling, however, and have never been sourcing, you may be at a loss as to how to find inventory. In this section, we'll cover some tips and tricks for navigating these sales and stores to find the best items to resell on Etsy.

Garage sales: Garage sales, also called *tag sales, rummage sales,* or *yard sales,* depending on the area, are often a great source of vintage items to resell on Etsy. You typically find garage sales listed in local newspapers, community bulletin boards, or even on social media platforms like Facebook. There are also websites such as YardSaleSearch.com, GarageSaleFinder.com, and gsalr.com where people advertise their sales.

I like to plan my garage sale route the night before using Google Maps. I make sure to bring plenty of cash, especially small bills, as most garage sales don't accept checks or credit cards. In my area, there are many people who don't even advertise their sales other than putting signs out. Sometimes I just drive around the area following signs to the sales!

Estate sales: Estate sales are a great source of vintage items to buy to resell on Etsy. Estate sales typically occur when the contents of a home are up for sale due to a homeowner passing away or downsizing to a nursing home. Estate sale companies are hired to manage the sale and clear out the contents of the home. At an estate sale, items are often priced where they were left in the house, and shoppers can browse through the home to find treasures. It's important to note that most estate sale companies do not negotiate prices on the first day of the sale but may offer discounts of up to 50% off on the second day. Some even drop to 75% off or offer fill-a-bag sales in the final hours.

To find estate sales in your area, check local newspapers, Facebook, and sites like estatesales.net. When you go to an estate sale, make sure to bring your own bags to carry your items and plenty of cash. Some estate sale companies may accept credit cards or checks, but it's always best to be prepared with cash just in case. It's important to be respectful and courteous to estate sale workers, as this can help build relationships that may pay off in the future if you are looking to do bulk buys.

Thrift stores: Thrift stores can be excellent source for vintage items to sell on Etsy, depending on the prices. Most thrift stores have a variety of items ranging from clothing to home decor, kitchenware, and even toys.

Many thrift stores receive donations daily, so if you are relying on thrift stores for inventory, it is important to check back frequently for new items. And because thrift store inventory is from donations, condition can be a major issue. Be sure to thoroughly examine each item before deciding if you want to purchase it for your Etsy shop.

Some thrift stores may have a designated vintage section, while others may mix vintage items in with the rest of the merchandise. Keep in mind that prices at thrift stores can vary widely. Some stores may have high prices on vintage items, while others may not realize the value of the items they have.

Church sales: Church sales can be a treasure trove of vintage items at bargain prices. Many times, church members will donate items that have been passed down through generations, including vintage clothing, jewelry, kitchenware, and decor. The proceeds from the sale typically go to support the church or other charitable causes.

Church sales can be advertised in local newspapers, community bulletin boards, church websites, and on social media sites. They are often held on weekends and are open to the public. When shopping at church sales, be sure to bring cash and small bills, as many of these sales do not accept credit cards. It's also a good idea to arrive early, as the best items tend to go quickly. Finally, be sure to be polite and respectful, as these sales are often staffed by volunteers from the church.

Flea markets: Flea markets are events where vendors sell secondhand goods, antiques, and vintage items. They are usually held outdoors, in large open spaces or parking lots. You can find flea markets by checking local newspapers and social media sites.

When shopping at a flea market, it's best to arrive early to get the best selection. Bring cash and small bills, as many vendors may not accept credit cards. It's also a good idea to bring a measuring tape and a bag or cart to carry your purchases.

Flea markets can be a great place to find vintage items to sell on Etsy, as vendors often have unique and rare pieces that can't be found in traditional retail stores. However, it's important to carefully inspect items before purchasing, as some vendors may try to pass off reproductions or fakes as vintage. It's also okay to negotiate prices with vendors, as many are willing to haggle to make a sale.

Antique malls: It may seem counterintuitive to shop at antique malls and antique stores for items to resell on Etsy. After all, items are usually priced at full retail price, leaving little to no room for profit on Etsy. However, visiting antique malls can be a great way to research what is currently trending so that you can seek it out elsewhere. I think of antique stores as price guidebooks where I can learn what the going rate for antiques and vintage items are.

However, you may still be able to find items to resell at these stores. I've stumbled upon antique mall booths that were having sales, even going-out-of-business sales, where I was able to snatch up great deals. If you encounter the shop or booth owner, be friendly and chat with them. Most people who sell at antique malls do not sell online as they are fearful of technology, but many times they are interested in the process. By making connections with these sellers, you may find opportunities to buy from them directly before they bring their items to their booth or to offer to buy in bulk from them from the inventory they have stored elsewhere.

Facebook Marketplace: Facebook Marketplace is a great resource for finding vintage items to sell on Etsy. To get started, you will need to have a Facebook account and navigate to the *Marketplace* tab. From there, you can search for specific vintage items or browse through different categories such as *Antiques, Collectibles,* and *Vintage.* You can also filter your search by location and price range.

One benefit of shopping on Facebook Marketplace is that you can often negotiate with the seller for a lower price. You can message the seller directly to ask questions about the item, negotiate the price, and arrange for payment and pickup. To be safe, arrange for pick up in a public place, not at your home or the home of the seller.

When shopping on Facebook Marketplace, be sure to carefully examine the item before making a purchase. Ask for additional photos if needed and inquire about any flaws or damage. Be prepared to negotiate, but also be respectful of the seller's asking price. And always make sure to arrange for safe and secure payment and pickup.

Online arbitrage: If you are lacking sourcing opportunities in your area, you can find inventory online on the very sites where you want to resell items. Savvy resellers are always souring Etsy, eBay, Poshmark, Mercari, and WhatNot in search of low-priced items than can buy to resell. Search out items in specific categories and change the search to show you the lowest priced items first. Be aware of shipping charges, though, as postage costs will eat into your profits.

Local auctions: Local auction houses can be a great place to find antiques to resell on Etsy. Many auctions houses these days are online only, although some still do in-person auctions. If you can attend a preview of the auction items, definitely go so you can see the condition of items in person. Be aware of auctioneer fees that are added to each sale and make sure you can pick up your purchases in the designated time frame. If you buy a lot, ensure you are able to load your purchases and have room in your vehicle for everything.

Word of mouth: Lastly, it's always a good idea to let your friends and family know that you're selling antiques and vintage collectibles on Etsy. Posting the occasional reminder on your Facebook page is a great way to remind your contacts that you are always buying vintage items for your business. You never know when someone may have items that they no longer need or want that they are willing to sell at a steep discount or even give them to you for free. I've had friends and family members reach out to me specifically to see if I was interested in certain items they found at garage sales or that they found in a relative's basement.

CHAPTER FIVE: OPENING AN ETSY SHOP

So far in this book, we have covered the benefits of selling antiques and vintage collectibles on Etsy as well as the various items you can sell (and those you cannot sell) on the platform. Assuming you have some items that you are ready to sell, the next step is to create a seller account and set up your Etsy shop. Don't worry: It's an easy process, and this chapter will walk you step by step through it.

If you're already an Etsy shopper, creating a seller account is a separate process that requires additional information in order for you to gain approval to sell products. You will still be logged in under your buyer account, so there will be no need to log in and out to either buy or sell. If you don't already have a buyer account, creating a seller account will automatically make one for you.

To set up an Etsy seller account, follow these steps:

1. Go to the **Etsy website** and click on the **Sell on Etsy** button.
2. Click the **Open your Etsy shop** button.
3. Enter your **email address** and **password** to create an account or sign in with an existing account. You can create your seller account under your buyer account, you'll just need to add some additional information.
4. Choose your **shop language** and **country**.
5. Enter your **shop name.**
6. Agree to **Etsy's terms of use and policies.**
7. Click the **Create your shop** button to complete the process.

Once you've completed the **Create Your Etsy Shop** process, the next step is to set up your **Shop Preferences**. You can always access your

Shop Manager by clicking on the store-shaped icon located at the top of all Etsy pages in your **Etsy Seller Dashboard**.

Keep in mind that you have the option to skip this step and return later to set up your shop preferences. And you can edit these settings at any time. In fact, most of your settings can be edited at any time, so you are never locked into any of your choices.

PRO TIP: I have my **Shop Manager** bookmarked on my desktop computer so that I can quickly access it to create new listings and manage my shop. I also have the **Etsy Seller App** installed on my phone so I can easily access my account from anywhere at any time. Being able to access my shop when I'm away from my office is important as it allows me to quickly answer any messages from buyers. Etsy is very strict about sellers answering questions from customers as quickly as possible; failing to do so in a timely manner can affect your seller status. So having the app on my phone allows me to respond to questions even when I am away from my office.

Etsy Shop Preferences are the settings that allow you to customize and manage various aspects of your Etsy shop. You can access your shop preferences by going to **Shop Manager** and clicking on the **Preferences** tab.

Here are some of the things you can do in your **Etsy Shop Preferences**:

- Set your shop location and language.
- Set your shop policies, such as your return policy.
- Customize your shop's appearance by adding a banner image and logo.
- Enable automatic renewal or manual renewal for your listings.
- Choose how you want to handle orders, including setting up automatic email responses.

- Set up Google Analytics to track your shop's performance.
- Set up shipping profiles to streamline the process of shipping your products.
- Enable or disable various features, such as the ability to offer gift wrapping or to allow customers to request custom orders.

Time Commitment: When you set up your shop on Etsy, the system will ask you how much time you plan to dedicate to it. This is just a way for Etsy to gather analytical information on sellers. You can select if selling on Etsy is your full-time or part-time gig, or you can skip the question altogether.

Shop Name: Selecting the name for your Etsy shop sets the tone for your business. It's one of the first things customers will see when they stumble across your store, so you want to make sure it's eye-catching, memorable, and accurately reflects your brand. Selecting your shop name is the first step in building your brand, so you want to make sure it reflects the items you plan to sell.

If you're already selling antiques locally or on other websites, you likely already have a business name that you're happy with. However, if someone else on Etsy is already using that name, you will have to create a different one. Search Etsy for the shop name you want to use to see what comes up. If yours is already taken, you can modify yours slightly. For instance, if your business is called "Ann's Antiques" and that name is taken, you could name your shop "Ann's Antiques & Vintage" or "Annie's Antiques."

Be sure that your shop name adheres to Etsy's naming guidelines and that it doesn't contain any prohibited words or phrases. Etsy has certain requirements and guidelines for shop names to ensure that they are appropriate and do not violate the platform's policies. Here are some of the main requirements and guidelines for shop names on Etsy:

- Shop names must be unique and not already in use by another Etsy seller.
- Shop names must not contain any prohibited words or phrases, such as offensive language or trademarked terms.
- Shop names must not imply that you are affiliated with Etsy or any other company or organization.
- Shop names must not contain any personal information, such as phone numbers or addresses.
- Shop names must not be too long or difficult to spell or pronounce.

- Shop names must be 4-20 characters in length.
- Shop names cannot contain spaces or special characters.
- Shop names cannot contain profanity.
- Shop names cannot infringe on another's trademark.

Set Up Payment & Billing: In the next step of setting up your Etsy shop, you will be required to provide payment and billing information. This includes entering a valid payment method that Etsy can use to charge you in case your fees exceed your sales.

Remember that when you sell something on Etsy, Etsy will automatically take out their fees and shipping costs before depositing the remaining balance in your Etsy account. If you have to process a refund or if your fees exceed your net profits, your Etsy balance could fall into the negative. At that time, Etsy would charge your credit card for any outstanding fees you've occurred.

When setting up your Etsy shop, you will also need to enter your bank account information so Etsy can pay you for your sales. To set up your Etsy shop's payment and billing, follow these steps:

1. Go to the **Shop Manager** and click on the **Finances** tab.

2. Etsy will prompt you to enter your bank account routing information for direct deposit.
3. Choose your **Deposit schedule** (every day, once a week, every two weeks, or once a month)
4. Click the **Save** button to save your payment settings.

Note that the information you need to provide to set up an Etsy seller account varies depending on the country you are registering in as well as if you are signing up as an **individual/sole proprietorship** or a **business entity**. If you're registering as an *individual/sole proprietor*, you will be required to furnish personal details like your name, contact information, and, if you're located in the United States, your social security number.

On the other hand, if you're registering with a *business entity*, specifically an *LLC*, you will need to provide more extensive information about your enterprise, such as its official name, contact information, and pertinent documentation.

Are you confused about the difference between a *sole proprietorship* and an *LLC*? Don't worry, many new sellers are. Here is an explanation of the difference between them:

A **sole proprietorship** is a business in which an individual is the sole owner and operator of the business. As a *sole proprietor*, the business owner has complete control over all aspects of their business and is personally responsible for all debts and liabilities. For tax purposes, the business is *not* considered a separate entity, and the owner reports all business income and expenses on their personal tax return. In the United States, a *sole proprietor* may use their Social Security number as their business identification number for tax purposes.

A **Limited Liability Company,** referred to as an **LLC,** also offers greater flexibility in terms of taxation. By default, an *LLC* is considered a "pass-through" entity, which means that the profits and losses of the business pass through to the owners' personal tax returns, and the business itself does not pay federal income taxes. However, *LLCs* can choose to be taxed as a corporation if they prefer.

Unlike a *sole proprietorship*, an *LLC* can have an unlimited number of owners. In terms of legal requirements, an *LLC* typically requires more paperwork and formalities than a *sole proprietorship*. This can include filing articles of organization with the state, creating an operating agreement, and obtaining any necessary licenses or permits. However, the exact requirements vary by state. Always check with a certified accountant for the rules in your area.

Most Etsy sellers, including myself, are *sole proprietors*. As explained above, being a *sole proprietor* simply means that I pay taxes as an individual, not a corporation, using my Social Security number and not a business license. I operate my Etsy shop as a one-person business and am not registered as a corporation or LLC with the government.

Note that the need for a business license varies by location; be sure to consult your county or with a local tax professional or CPA to learn the laws for your area.

When registering your business on Etsy, you will need to provide specific information on the **How you'll get paid** page during the setup process of your shop, including:

- Your full legal name and contact information including address and phone number
- Your social security number (for United States citizens) or your taxpayer identification number (TIN)
- Your bank account information, including the bank name, routing number, and account number. You can find your routing and account numbers at the bottom of your checks.

Note that this information isn't just for how you will get paid, but also for tax purposes. There is no way to get around giving Etsy this information. Every online selling platform, including Amazon, eBay, Poshmark, Mercari, and even Facebook Marketplace requires this information to sell on their websites. Online sales are income, and you have to report your income to the government and pay taxes on your earnings.

Test Deposit: After you have provided your payment and billing information, Etsy will initiate a *test deposit*, which is simply a verification process to ensure the accuracy of your payment information and to confirm that you can receive payouts. This process involves Etsy issuing you a small deposit, typically less than a dollar, to your bank account. You are not required to repay this test deposit.

To complete the verification process, you will need to check your bank account to locate the *test deposit* and confirm that you have received it. You simply enter the amount of the *test deposit* on the *How you'll get paid* page to finalize the verification process. Note that Etsy will remind you to complete this process and provide you with the prompts to do so.

The *test deposit* may take a few days to appear in your bank account, so don't panic if you don't see it immediately. If you have any issues with the verification process, you can contact Etsy's support team for assistance. You can easily contact Etsy support at any time and for any reason by following these steps:

1. Go to **www.etsy.com** and click the **Help & Policies** tab at the bottom of the page.
2. Scroll down to the **Contacting Etsy** section and click the **Contact Us** button.
3. Select the appropriate **category** for your issue from the dropdown menu.

4. Enter a **subject** and a **detailed description** of your issue in the provided fields.
5. Click the **Continue** button to submit your request.

Etsy support typically responds within 24 hours, although it can take longer during peak times.

Two-Factor Authentication: *Two-factor authentication* is an additional security measure that requires you to provide a verification code when signing in from an unrecognized browser or device. This helps to protect your account from unauthorized access and ensures that only you can access your Etsy shop. More and more businesses, including banks, social media platforms, and e-commerce websites are encouraging users to implement *two-factor authentication* to protect their accounts.

To set up *two-factor authentication*, you will need to choose a method for receiving your verification code. Etsy allows you to receive your verification code in one of three ways:

1. **Text message:** If you choose this option, you will receive a text message with your verification code whenever you need to sign in from an unrecognized browser or device.
2. **Authenticator app:** If you choose this option, you will need to download an authenticator app on your phone and use it to generate your verification code whenever you need to sign in from an unrecognized browser or device.
3. **Email:** If you choose this option, you will receive an email with your verification code whenever you need to sign in from an unrecognized browser or device.

Note that you want to use a communication method you always have access to. I choose my authentications to come to me via text message as I always have my phone nearby. I find this method the easiest and fastest way to log in.

Set Up Your Storefront: Once you've gotten through entering your personal and banking information, verifying your account, and setting up *two-factor authorization,* you can move on to the fun step of designing your Etsy shop storefront!

Creating an Etsy seller account automatically gives you an Etsy shop. It isn't something you need to manually "open" or apply for; it's instantly there for you after you have set up your account.

To set up your Etsy shop storefront, follow these steps (note that we'll go over these options more in-depth later in this chapter):

1. Go to your Etsy seller dashboard and click the **Shop settings** tab.
2. Click the **Shop info & Appearance** tab on the left side of the page.
3. Enter a **shop title** and **shop announcement** that will appear at the top of your shop's homepage.
4. Add a **shop banner** image that will appear at the top of your shop's homepage.
5. Add a **shop icon**, which is a small image that will represent your shop on Etsy.
6. Enter a **shop description** that will appear on your shop's homepage and in search results.
7. Click the **Save** button to save your changes.

As I mentioned earlier, all Etsy sellers are automatically given an Etsy store. However, there are two different options available to you, *Etsy Standard* and *Etsy Plus.*

Etsy Standard: *Etsy Standard* is the default level of shop access for all sellers on the platform. Signing up to sell on Etsy automatically gets you an *Etsy Standard* shop, which offers all of the basic features and functions necessary for selling on Etsy. There is no additional charge for an *Etsy Standard* shop; the only upfront cost is the listing fee of $0.20 per item, charged when you create a new listing or relist an expired one. The fee covers four months, meaning you can list one item on Etsy for one year for only $.60. Remember that final value fees apply once an item sells, but those fees are automatically deducted from your balance along with postage costs if you print your shipping labels through Etsy.

Etsy Plus: *Etsy Plus* is a paid subscription shop plan that provides sellers with advanced features and tools beyond what is included in the basic *Etsy Standard* plan. For a monthly fee of $10, *Etsy Plus* members receive listing 15 credits and $5 in credit towards *Etsy Ads,* as well as access to advanced shop appearance options, a custom domain name, and Etsy's wholesale platform.

Note that *Etsy Plus* offers a discount on *Hover* domains, although sellers can choose to purchase a domain from other providers such as *GoDaddy.* Once you have settled on your business name, I recommend locking the domain name in before someone else claims it. I own the domains for several variations of my name, all of which point to my *Amazon Author Page* where my books are located. I also have domains that point to my eBay and Etsy stores.

Etsy Plus subscribers have the option to enable *Restock requests* in their listings, which allows interested shoppers to view your sold-out listings and to sign up to receive an alert when items are back in stock. While this feature is geared towards shops that sell re-stockable inventory, such as supplies and crafts, it can also be helpful for antique sellers as it can give insight into what collectibles to source and list for interested customers. For example, if you sell out of a particular figurine and see it has restock requests, you will know to specifically look for that piece when out sourcing. And since there is interest in it, you might be able to charge more once you get more listed.

And finally, *Etsy Plus* subscribers have access to discounts and perks such as savings on custom shipping boxes, business cards, and other promotional materials. However, I personally find better prices on shipping supplies, including enclosures, elsewhere. I buy shipping supplies on Amazon and at Sam's Club. And I purchase enclosure stickers and magnets from a site called Sticker Mule.

Featured Items: Featured items are listings or shop sections that are prominently displayed on a seller's shop page. All sellers on Etsy, both *Standard* and *Plus*, have the **standard grid** option, which allows you to feature up to four listings or shop sections on your shop's page.

Etsy Plus subscribers, however, have the additional option to use a **mixed grid layout.** With a mixed grid layout, *Etsy Plus* subscribers can feature one big listing or shop section along with four smaller items or shop sections on their shop page. Basically, *Etsy Plus* gives you a few more design options with your shop's layout.

While you do not have to enable these grid options, if you do, be sure to carefully select the items or sections you want to feature as they will be the first thing buyers see when they visit your Etsy shop. Make sure you keep them up to date and in season. For example, if you selected Easter items to be highlighted during the spring, don't forget to change them out after Easter is over. Leaving up outdated featured items gives the appearance that you don't care about your shop, which can make customers think you won't care about their orders. It is better not to use grids than to leave stale arrangements up.

Should you start your Etsy shop with *Etsy Standard* or upgrade to *Etsy Plus*? That is a choice only you can make. Most sellers start with *Etsy*

Standard and then upgrade to *Etsy Plus* as their business grows. The listing and ad credits, the customization options, the advanced shop management, the promotional tools, and the priority customer support are, in my opinion, all well worth the $10 monthly fee. And since you pay on a month-to-month basis, you can cancel your subscription at any time and revert to *Etsy Standard*. If, later on, you decide you want to go back to *Etsy Plus*, you can easily reactivate your membership.

Number of listings: When you sell online, regardless of the platform you sell on or what items you sell, having as many items listed as possible will give you the best chance of making sales. If you only have a handful of antiques listed in your Etsy shop, it will be hard to make sales. However, by listing as many sellable items as you can, you will have an easier time attracting buyers. Again, it only costs $.60 to list an item for one year on Etsy, which means you could list 100 items for only $80 for a year. That's far less than what most antique malls charge you to have a booth!

PRO TIP: I recommend having a wide variety of different price ranges in your Etsy shop. While we all want those high-dollar sales, if you offer some lower-priced items, you will have a better chance of making consistent sales while you wait for the right customers to find your more expensive offerings. Frequent sales, even if they are small, keep your store active. And Etsy, like most selling platforms, favors active shops. If Etsy's system sees that your shop is making sales, it will begin to push your listings to the top of the search algorithm, which will lead to more sales.

Etsy Shop Icon: Your Etsy *shop icon*, also known as your logo or profile picture, is a small image that serves as the visual representation of your shop on the Etsy platform. It appears alongside your shop name on your shop's homepage, on your listings, and on various other pages on the Etsy website and app.

Your *shop icon* is a crucial component of your branding and should ideally be used across all your social media platforms to maintain consistency and brand recognition. This means that your Etsy shop icon should be the same profile picture on every website where your business has a presence. This will make it easier for customers to recognize your brand on whatever platform they are on. Since some online sellers have similar names, sometimes it's the profile picture that will end up separating you from other businesses when people are searching for you online.

To set up your **Etsy shop icon**, you will need to follow these steps:

1. Sign into your Etsy account and go to the **Shop Manager** section.
2. Click on **Settings** and then click on the **Info & Appearance** tab.
3. Scroll down to the **Shop Icon** section and click on the **Change Icon** button.
4. Select the image you want to use as your shop icon from your computer or device. The image must be at least 500 x 500 pixels and in a .jpg, .gif, or .png format.
5. Click on the **Save** button to apply your changes.

If you don't already have a logo or icon for your business, you can use a site like Fiverr.com to hire a graphic designer to create one for you. For around $10, you can have someone create a professional-looking graphic that will represent your business on Etsy, promotional materials, and social media.

Shop Story: An *Etsy shop story* is where you can share a summary of your shop's products, your overall brand, your business goals, and a bit about you as a person. Connecting with shoppers in this way shows them you are a real person, which can go a long way toward your customers feeling like they know you. And people are more inclined to buy from someone they have a connection with.

To set up your **Etsy shop story** follow these steps:

1. Sign into your Etsy account and click on the **Shop Manager** button in the top right corner of the page.
2. Click on the **Settings** tab and then click on the **About Your Shop** tab.
3. Click on the **Story tab** at the top of the page.
4. Enter in a **Story Headline.**
5. Fill in the **Story** field.
6. You can also add a **Shop Video** here.
7. You can also add in **Shop Photos**.
8. You can also **add links to your social media pages**.
9. Click on the **Save** button to apply your changes.
10. You can edit or delete any of these sections any time after you create them.

Etsy Shop Title & Shop Announcement: The *Shop Title* and *Shop Announcement* can spruce up your Etsy shop's storefront as they appear at the top of your shop's homepage, meaning they are the first sections customers will see when visiting your shop. Note that both of these sections can be edited at any time, or you can choose to leave them blank.

If you do decide to include a *Shop Title*, it should be a short phrase that represents your store and the products you offer. On the other hand, your *Shop Announcement* is a longer paragraph or two that can be used to share important time-sensitive information with your customers, such as new product launches, promotions, or updated policies. Think of a *Shop Title* as a headline with a *Shop Announcement* being the article.

To create a *Shop Title,* choose a phrase that accurately reflects your shop's products and style. I have an Etsy sticker shop where the *Shop Title* is *Retro & Vintage Inspired Stickers & Magnets.* For the *Shop Announcement,* craft a message that is informative and engaging, and consider adding relevant keywords to maximize your Etsy SEO or *Search Engine Optimization.* We will cover Etsy SEO extensively later in this book, but for now just know that it involves repeating the most important keywords for your listing in the title, description, tags, and shop section.

My *Shop Announcement* for my sticker shop is *Welcome to Jean Lee Publishing! We specialize in vinyl waterproof stickers and magnets that are perfect for water bottles, laptops, refrigerators, cars, crafting, and gifting. All items ship for FREE from Iowa the following business day after orders are placed, with USPS tracking immediately uploaded for your convenience.*

To access your *Shop Title* and *Shop Announcement* sections, click on the **Settings** tab in your **Shop Manager** and then click on **Info & Appearance.** Again, you can change these areas at any time or leave them blank until you have built up your shop and are more comfortable filling them out.

Message to Buyers: Also under the *Info & Appearance* section is a space to write a message to your buyers that Etsy will automatically include on receipt pages and in the email they send to buyers whenever they place an order on the site. A simple *thank you for your order* message with a general statement about shipping times is enough to include here. My message reads, *Thank you for your order! We appreciate your business! Once your order has shipped (typically the next business day) the tracking information will automatically be uploaded for your convenience.* However, you can leave this section blank and Etsy will send customers a generic notification of their order.

Etsy Shop Banner: An Etsy *shop banner* is a large image that appears at the top of your shop's homepage and gives potential customers an idea of what your shop is all about. Just as with your *Shop Title* and *Shop Announcement*, your banner image is an important element of your shop's appearance, as it helps create a professional and cohesive look for your shop. And while you don't have to have a shop banner, your shop will look much better with one.

To edit your Etsy Banner, first, log into your **Shop Manager**. Then **click on the pencil icon next to your shop's name,** which is under **SALES CHANNELS** on the left-hand side of the page. This will bring up a page where you can edit your shop's banner.

Just as you want your Etsy **shop icon** to be cohesive across all of your social media platforms, you want to do the same with your banner. Facebook and YouTube both allow banners, and it's easy to place your Etsy banner on both of those sites. You can create a banner using Canva or pay to have one created for you on a site such as Fiverr or UpWork.

Etsy Plus subscribers have access to four different banner styles:

- **Carousel** allows you to show off multiple photos, one at a time, which you can link to listings or sections.
- **Collage** allows you to combine up to four photos in a collage.
- **Big Banner** allows you to fill the top of your shop with one image that you can link to a listing or section.
- **Mini Banner** allows you to add a visual pop while keeping the focus on your listings.

Mixed Grid: All Etsy shops have the option to use a *Standard Grid* but *Etsy Plus* shops can also choose a *Mixed Grid* option that features five listings or shop sections with a couple of layout choices.

To edit your grid options, first, log into your **Shop Manager**. Then **click on the pencil icon next to your shop's name**. This will bring up a page where you can edit your shop's **Featured Items** with your grid options. Some sellers change their grid options every day to ensure returning customers are always greeted with a new look. However, most sellers opt to change them once a week or once a month.

Hiring out design services: When building your shop on Etsy, you want to use consistent graphics across not only in your store but all of your social media platforms to create a cohesive company image. Yes, even if you are only a one-person shop, you still want to present yourself as a company! If you aren't able to design your logos and banners yourself, or you simply don't have the time to create them, you can hire graphic designers to do the work for you.

There are several places where you can hire a designer to create your Etsy shop logo and banners, along with all graphics for your social media pages. Some options include:

1. **Fiverr:** Fiverr is an online marketplace where you can find freelance designers who offer a wide range of design services, including logo and banner design. You can browse through portfolios and reviews to find a designer who meets your needs and budget. It's easy to find a designer for under $10, especially new designers on the site who are eager to build their portfolios. I recommend choosing designers that offer at least two revisions of your order to ensure you get exactly what you want. A simple search of the "Etsy logo" or "Etsy banner" will get you started in your search.

2. **Upwork:** Upwork is another online marketplace where you can find freelance designers for hire. You can post a job listing and receive proposals from designers who are interested in working with you. You will likely pay more for a designer on

UpWork versus Fiverr, but the quality may also be better. Just like new designers on Fiverr charge less, you may find new designers on UpWork who are willing to do the job for less money to build their portfolio. As with Fiverr, I recommend choosing designers that offer at least two revisions. And try to find a designer who offers packages where you can get not only your Etsy graphics but all of the graphics you will need for your social media pages.

3. **99designs:** 99designs is a design contest platform where you can hold a design contest to receive multiple design options for your logo, icons, and banners. You can choose the design you like best and work with the designer to make any necessary revisions.

4. **Etsy:** You can also find designers on Etsy who offer design services, including logo and banner design.

5. **Friends & Family:** You can seek your local graphic design recommendations on Facebook. You never know who your friends and family may know that do the kind of work you are looking to hire out.

Shop Options: You can find **Options** under the **Settings** tab in your shop managers. Etsy allows you to pre-determine several options for your store, including:

Rearrange Your Shop: Enabling this feature will show shop visitors the *Custom* sort option by default. Or you can disable this feature so that shop visitors will see the *Most Recently Listed* sort option by default.

Custom Order Requests: If you are offering custom or personalized products, you can enable a setting where a *Request Custom Order* button will appear across your shop. The vast majority of antique sellers do not offer to personalize items, so you will want to disable this feature so customers know that the products you are selling are as pictured.

Offer Gift Wrapping: Etsy allows sellers to offer gift wrapping services to their buyers. Think long and hard before offering gift wrap as customers will expect items to be wrapped as they would be in a luxury department store setting. Wrapping items will add time to your process and will cost you more in supplies.

However, if you do want to offer gift wrapping, Etsy allows you to set your price for buyers to pay. Your gift options will then appear on every listing (except for digital products).

I have never offered gift wrapping. When buyers ask, I simply explain that to ensure their items arrive safely that I do not gift wrap them but rather take care in packaging them with clean packing materials.

Offer Gift Message: While gift wrapping can be a costly and time-consuming service, enabling the ability for customers to include a gift message with their order is free and easy to do. If your buyer chooses to include a gift message, it will print on a sheet of paper that you can fold into a gift card. Note that if a customer includes a gift message that the packing slip will print without the price of the item showing.

PRO TIP: Sometimes customers will contact you after they have paid for the order and ask you to send the package to a different address. Maybe they forgot to update their address or they want it sent as a gift. Note that if you change the address, the order will no longer qualify for *Etsy Seller Protection*. In these cases, I offer to cancel the order and instruct the customer to repurchase the item with the correct shipping address.

Automatic Listing Translation: In today's global marketplace, reaching a diverse range of customers is essential for the success of your Etsy shop. Even if you primarily focus on domestic sales within the country you live in, it's important to remember that not everyone may speak your country's native language. As an American Etsy seller, I know that not all shoppers in the United States are fluent in English. By enabling Etsy's automatic translation feature, my listings are open to speakers of numerous languages around the world without me having to do any translation on my end.

Sold Listings: You can choose to let other Etsy users see your sold listings, or you can hide them. Some sellers choose to hide their sold listings so that competitors won't see them, but I personally don't see the logic in this. When you sell antiques, each piece is unique and has its own unique selling price. The choice to show or hide your sold listings is entirely up to you, however. If you choose to show them but later want to hide them, you can easily edit this section.

Current Time Zone: Etsy asks you to set your shop's time zone here. This is helpful when you are shipping orders as it lets customers know where you are located in relation to them so that they will have a better idea of how long shipping may take. It also helps let customers know why you may be taking a while to answer their message. After all, it might be daytime for them but nighttime for you. I am located in Iowa in the Central Time Zone; if a customer on the other side of the world messages me when it is noon for them, they can see that it is the middle of the night for me.

Vacation Mode: If you ever need to put your Etsy shop on vacation (whether because you are taking an actual vacation or are simply unable to process orders), you can easily put your entire store on vacation so that customers cannot purchase anything from your store. In fact, while your storefront will still be visible, your listings will be hidden. You can also include a *Vacation Announcement* that will display at the top of your shop. And you can write up a *Messages Autoreply*, which will be sent to anyone who sends you a message while your *Vacation Mode* is on.

To put your Etsy shop on vacation:

1. Log into your **Shop Manager**
2. Click on **Settings**
3. Click on **Options**
4. Click on the **Vacation Mode** tab
5. Select **ON Your shop is on vacation**
6. To turn **Vacation Mode** off, simply log back in and select **OFF Your shop is active**

It's good to know how to quickly put your shop on vacation not only on your computer but also on your smartphone in case of an emergency. You also want to make sure someone close to you knows how to turn vacation mode on, too, in the event you are unable to do it yourself . The last thing you want is for orders to pile up unfulfilled, which will cause Etsy to eventually cancel those orders, issue refunds to your customers, and put a strike against your account. I've had situations where I was in the hospital emergency room and had to use my phone to put my shop on vacation as I wasn't going to be home in time to process orders according to my handling time.

Download Data: The *Download Data* section in your *Etsy Seller Dashboard* allows you to download various types of data about your Etsy shop in CSV (Comma Separated Value) format. Here is a breakdown of the different options available:

1. **Orders:** This option allows you to download data about your shop's orders, including order ID, date, buyer information, order status, and item details.
2. **Listings:** This option allows you to download data about

your shop's listings, including listing ID, title, description, price, quantity, and other relevant details.

3. **Finances:** This option allows you to download data about your shop's finances, including revenue, fees, taxes, and payment information.

4. **Shop:** This option allows you to download data about your shop's settings and preferences, including shop names, policies, and shipping information.

5. **Web Analytics:** This option allows you to download data about your shop's web analytics, including visits, views, conversion rates, revenue, traffic sources, and search terms.

By downloading this data, you can analyze it using spreadsheet software like Microsoft Excel or Google Sheets and gain deeper insights into your shop's performance. You can also use this data to create custom reports and visualizations that can help you make informed decisions about how to optimize your shop and drive more sales.

Knowing where your shop traffic is coming from tells you where you need to focus your marketing efforts. If you get a steady stream of customers from Etsy but not your social media accounts, you will know you need to work on building those sites up. But if all of your traffic is coming from social media and not Etsy, you may need to work on your SEO (which we will cover extensively later in this book) or run Etsy ads.

Close Shop: Also under the *Options* section is a tab to close your Etsy shop. Note that if you have *Etsy Standard,* you only pay when you list an item. So, there is no reason to close your shop if you simply aren't listing new products. If you have an *Etsy Plus* account, you can simply cancel the $10 monthly subscription and leave your shop as is, even if there are no listings, just in case you want to come back to it in the future. Remember that you can change the name of your shop at any time, so if you rebrand, you can easily change the name, look, and policies to fit a different business model. That way you don't have to cancel your current shop, you can simply rebrand it.

Shipping Policies: The shipping settings section of your Etsy account (accessible under the *Settings* tab) is where you can manage and configure the shipping options for your shop. Note that you can create shipping profiles within each of your listings to match up with the various products you are selling. We'll be covering shipping in depth later in this book.

Policy Settings: Also under the *Settings* section is where you can create your *Policy Settings.* Here you can set up the following:

Returns & Exchanges: Etsy allows sellers to set their own policies for returns and exchanges on their products. Most antique sellers do not allow for returns or exchanges unless an item is not as described in the listing. For instance, if you listed a set of vintage flatware as sterling silver when in fact it was silverplated, that is a mistake on your part and you need to accept the return. However, if a customer simply doesn't like an item once they received it, that is a mistake on their part.

As a seller, you want to do everything in your power to prevent return requests from happening. Make sure your photos are clear and your descriptions are accurate. Most vintage items show some wear due to age and storage. Don't ever promise customers that something you are selling is in mint condition. If anything, downplay the condition so as not to get the buyer's hopes up.

Cancellations: The cancellations setting on Etsy allows sellers to set their policies for canceling orders. These policies can vary from seller to seller and can include information on the conditions under which a buyer can cancel an order and any fees that may be associated with the cancellation.

It is considered good customer service to allow customers to cancel an order shortly after they place it. Sometimes a buyer may have simply made a mistake and will contact you within minutes of placing their order. I personally just agree to cancel these orders. Setting a timeframe for which you will accept cancellations is important to let buyers know they have a short window of time to request a cancellation.

Production Partners: Etsy shops that sell print-on-demand, crafts, or digital products often use third-party resources to help create their products, which they need to disclose as *Production Partners*. Sellers of antiques and vintage items do not utilize *Production Partners*, so you can skip this section.

Facebook Shops: *Facebook Shops* is another feature under the *Settings* tab on the Etsy seller dashboard that enables you to connect your Etsy shop with your Facebook account and establish a store on Facebook. This will allow you to sell your products directly on Facebook, in addition to your Etsy shop.

When you connect your Etsy shop to Facebook, you can easily transfer your products, product information, and inventory to your Facebook store. Furthermore, once connected, you can sync your inventory and sales across both platforms, so you don't have to worry about managing stock levels or order fulfillment between the two.

It is important to note that you will need to have a Facebook business page, not just a personal account, set up before creating a store and linking it to your Etsy shop. We will discuss creating a Facebook page for your business later in this book.

Community & Help: You can keep up with all of Etsy's official news releases and seller announcements as well as get help under the *Community & Help* section, which is linked in your *Shop Manager.* You can also access the *Help Center* from any Etsy page directly on the site by scrolling down to the very bottom and locating the *Help* section.

Etsy will try to direct you first to one of their *frequently asked questions* sections, but if you can't find what you need, you can initiate contact with them via email, chat, or phone by clicking on the **Contact Etsy Support** button at the bottom of the *Help* page.

Etsy Fees: We touched on Etsy selling fees a bit earlier in this book, but we will go over them in depth now so you know how much money you will be spending to sell on the platform:

Listing Fees: Etsy charges a $.20 fee to list an item for four months. This $.20 fee is charged whenever you create a new listing or relist an expired one. Note that this fee is for one LISTING. You may list several items within one listing if you have different variations of it. For example, in my Etsy sticker shop, I sell matte stickers, holographic stickers, and magnets of the same design. I can create one listing for each design but offer all three options under each listing. I don't pay for each variation. I only pay the $.20 fee for the single listing.

While no one likes to pay fees, the $.20 listing fee on Etsy is quite low, especially when compared to other e-commerce sites like Amazon or eBay. At the end of the four months, you can opt to renew the listing for another four months at the same cost of $0.20, making the total cost to list one item for a full year on Etsy only $.60.

Transaction Fees: In addition to the $.20 listing fee, Etsy also charges a transaction fee on each sale that you make. Like their low listing fees, this 5% transaction fee on Etsy is a small price to pay for the exposure and resources provided by the platform, including payment processing and the ability to print shipping labels right from your account. The transaction fee is calculated on the sale price of each item, including shipping and, if any, gift-wrapping charges.

Payment Processing Fees: Etsy makes it easy for customers to pay using a variety of methods as it partners with different payment processors to handle transactions, and these processors charge various fees for their services. This fee is typically around 2.9% + $.30 per transaction, which allows customers to pay for their orders using their debit cards, credit cards, or even PayPal. If you had to arrange payment processing yourself, it would cost much more. Not only does Etsy handle the payments from buyers, but they also handle the distribution of your profits to your bank account. And they collect and remit sales tax to the states that mandate it.

When I started selling online in 2005 on eBay, getting paid was sometimes quite an adventure, to say the least. Back then, PayPal was the primary payment system used by eBay, and some customers were hesitant to trust the site. I had customers mail me checks and sometimes even cash through the mail to pay for their orders!

Fortunately, payment processing is now integrated into all online selling platforms, including Etsy. Thanks to *Etsy Payments*, I don't have to worry about collecting payments from my customers. Buyers can pay for their orders using different methods, such as credit and debit cards, PayPal, and gift cards. Etsy handles the payment processing, holding the funds in escrow until the seller confirms the shipment of the order. This means that there's no need for sellers to send invoices or chase down payments, as everything is automated through Etsy. I don't ever see how my customers paid, I only see the profits deposited into my account.

Advertising & Promotional Fees: In addition to the listing and payment processing fees, Etsy offers various advertising and promotional options for sellers who want to increase the visibility of their products. These options come with additional fees, which vary depending on the specific advertising or promotion being used.

Sales Tax: Selling on Etsy comes with a key advantage of the platform handling state sales tax collection and remittance on behalf of its sellers. This saves sellers a significant amount of time and effort as we don't have to collect and remit sales tax individually to each state, a requirement in most American states for online orders. This benefit of selling on Etsy is a major factor in why many sellers opt to keep their shop on the platform instead of setting up their own Shopify store. In fact, I have met successful Etsy shop owners who expanded to Shopify only to eventually go back to selling exclusively on Etsy for the sales tax collection alone!

Etsy Ads: Just listing products for sale on Etsy may not be enough to get customers to find your items. That's where *Etsy Ads* come in. *Etsy Ads* is an advertising program that lets you promote your products right on the Etsy site.

To get started with *Etsy Ads,* just head to your **Seller Dashboard**, click on the **Marketing** tab, and select **Etsy Ads**. Keep in mind that you have to pay every time someone clicks on your ad, regardless of whether or not they make a purchase. If you want to test Etsy ads, I recommend starting with a $5 daily budget for a month to see how your ads perform. You can adjust your budget at any time to fit your needs or you can cancel the ad if you aren't seeing results.

Etsy Offsite Ads: Unlike regular *Etsy Ads*, which are only shown on Etsy and for which you have to pay every time someone clicks on your ad, *Etsy Offsite Ads* offer sellers a chance to expand their reach beyond the Etsy marketplace and potentially increase sales by showcasing their products to shoppers on Google and other search engine sites. To enable this feature, go to your *Seller Dashboard*, click on the *Settings* tab, and select *Offsite Ads*.

If you sell less than $10,000 in a year on Etsy, you can choose whether or not to enable *Etsy Offsite Ads*. However, if you exceed $10,000 in annual sales, *Offsite Ads* are mandatory. Etsy will automatically enroll you in the program and you have no way to opt out. However, remember that since you only pay for the ad when someone orders something from you, there is no risk to the program.

PRO TIP: Because I focus heavily on Etsy SEO, I don't run regular *Etsy Ads* as I can get organic traffic from customers using the site. However, I do make sure I have opted into the *Offsite Ads* program as I want to participate even if my sales don't reach $10,000 within the calendar year. Again, I only pay for an offsite advertisement when it leads to a sale. To me, *Offsite Ads* are essentially free advertising for me as they bring people to my shop. If they make a purchase, I am then charged a small fee, which is easily covered by the money I made with the sale. Running my own Google Ads would cost a fortune, so the *Etsy Offsite Ads* program is a great benefit for me.

Seller Protection: Etsy provides several protections for sellers on its platform, including:

Payment Protection: With Etsy Payments, buyers' funds are securely held until the order has been completed and the package has been delivered. This is why it is so important to ship your orders through Etsy so that tracking will automatically upload. When you buy and print your shipping labels on Etsy, both you and your customer will be given the package's unique tracking number. If the package is lost, you can file a claim through Etsy to refund the buyer and be reimbursed for your costs.

Dispute Resolution: Etsy's dispute resolution process is designed to help sellers and buyers resolve issues in a fair and timely manner. The process can involve either mediation, where Etsy acts as a mediator to facilitate communication between the parties, or arbitration, where Etsy makes a final decision on the dispute.

Both sellers and buyers can get help resolving any disputes through **Etsy's Help section.** Simply **scroll down to the bottom of any Etsy page** and locate the **Help** heading. Underneath, click on **Help Center.**

When possible, do your best to resolve customer issues on your own. When you sell antiques and vintage collectibles, the condition is always an issue. As previously noted, you want to undersell the condition of the items you sell. Never say an item that is 20 years or older is in mint or perfect condition. And never claim it as new. Rather, you can describe items that are unopened in their original packaging with little wear as "new old stock."

However, if a customer simply has buyer's remorse, be kind but firm in your response. Making sure you have a strict "no returns or exchanges" policy is vital to protect yourself from unwarranted return requests. If you did everything right on your end, Etsy will likely back you in a customer dispute.

Often a customer who is pushing for a refund will balk if you offer for them to return the item. I find that they actually do want the item but are trying to get at least a partial refund, likely because they spent more than they should have. If the item has a tiny issue, you can always offer a small partial refund to see if that appeases the customer. Sometimes even a refund of a few dollars is enough to diffuse the situation.

Seller Protection Insurance: Etsy's *Seller Protection Insurance* is a program that provides coverage for eligible sellers. Here's how it works:

When you sell a product on Etsy, you're automatically enrolled in Etsy's *Seller Protection* program. If a buyer files a case against you for an item that was not as described, or if the item was damaged or lost during shipping, you may be eligible for reimbursement or protection through the program.

To be eligible for *Seller Protection*, however, you must meet certain requirements, such as providing accurate descriptions and photos of your products, shipping orders promptly, and resolving any issues with buyers promptly. Your account must be in good standing to qualify for this protection, so be sure to ship your orders promptly and quickly respond to messages, as Etsy looks at both of these when rating your shop.

If you're eligible for *Seller Protection*, Etsy may reimburse you for the cost of the item, shipping, and other associated costs, up to a maximum amount. The amount of coverage and the specific terms of the program may vary depending on the circumstances of the case.

It's important to note that *Seller Protection* is not a guarantee and may not cover all cases or circumstances. It's also important to take steps to protect yourself as a seller, such as using tracking and delivery confirmation, purchasing insurance for high-value items, and providing excellent customer service.

Maintaining *SELLER PROTECTION* eligibility is just one more reason why you want to keep all messaging through Etsy's system and why you want to print your shipping labels through their site. Keeping all communications and purchases through Etsy will protect you. If you want Etsy to have your back, you need to make sure you can prove that you did everything right on your end.

PRO TIP: If a buyer contacts you claiming an item hasn't been delivered but tracking shows it has, direct them to file a claim directly through Etsy. They can do this by clicking directly on their order and following the prompts on the screen. This removes you from the dispute process and puts the burden on Etsy directly to resolve the issue.

Shop Sections: *Shop Sections,* also referred to as your *store categories,* allow you to group your products into easy-to-navigate categories. This makes it simple for customers to find what they're looking for and for you to manage your inventory and listings more effectively. It also helps you sell more products as Etsy will offer other items in your shop sections to customers who are making a purchase. If someone is buying a piece of Depression glass from you and it was listed in your *Depression Glass* shop section, Etsy will show the customer other pieces you have listed, which may result in them adding on to their order.

To set up your Shop Sections, go to your **Seller Dashboard** and click on the **Listings** tab. On the right-hand side of the page will be the heading **Sections** with a drop-down menu underneath. Click on **Manage** to add and rearrange your shop categories. I personally like to arrange mine in alphabetical order.

Creating sections based on your different categories, niches, or special occasions and holidays will help customers easily narrow down the search results in your store. For example, if your shop is entirely devoted to vintage Christmas, you could create shop sections for each category you are selling such as *Christmas Ornaments, Christmas Figurines,* and *Christmas Ephemera.*

PRO TIP: I've mentioned Etsy SEO a few times now and will do so several more times in this book. This is because it is so important to the success of your shop. Remember that Etsy's SEO, or *search engine optimization,* is the single most important aspect of selling on the platform. When you create a listing, it's vital to repeat relevant keywords in the title, description, tags, and shop sections to help your item appear in search results.

For example, let's use the vintage Christmas shop example. You are listing a vintage set of ceramic Christmas angel figurines. You would want to include *vintage Christmas figurines* in the title and description.

You would want to create tags for *vintage Christmas*, *Christmas figurines*, and *vintage figurines*. And you would want to have a shop section for *Christmas Figurines*. Repeating these important keywords throughout your listing signals to Etsy that these are the keywords they need to focus on when showing your listing in search, which will lead to more shoppers seeing your listings.

CHAPTER SIX: CREATING ETSY LISTINGS

Once you have set up your Etsy account and shop, it's time to start listing your antiques for sale! If you're new to selling online, it's normal to feel a bit nervous as you set out to create your first listing. But don't worry, in this chapter, I'll guide you step-by-step through the entire process. As you gain more experience, creating new listings will become easier and faster. These days I can create an Etsy listing in under a minute with one eye closed!

Before we dive into creating your first listing, I want to again emphasize the importance of Etsy **Search Engine Optimization**, or **SEO**. I know, I know; you are probably sick of me talking about it. However, I cannot stress to you enough that the success of your Etsy shop is dependent on maximizing SEO. And just like creating new listings becomes easier with time, so does SEO.

To reiterate, SEO involves repeating important keywords in your listing title, description, tags, and shop sections. Unlike other e-commerce platforms where you only need to focus on loading keywords into listing titles, on Etsy it's essential to repeat keywords as much as possible. By repeating the most important keywords, you signal to Etsy that those are the terms they should prioritize when displaying your listings to customers.

Figuring out the most important keywords for each of your listings can be done with the help of keyword research tools such as EtsyCheck.com or eRank.com. As an example, let's say you are listing a vintage glass swung vase. If you type *swung vase* into EtsyCheck.com, you will be presented with a list of keywords ranked from the most searched to the least, including:

- Swung vase
- Vintage
- MCM
- Vintage glass
- Fenton
- LE Smith
- Vintage swung vase
- Vintage vase
- Viking glass
- Glass
- Vase
- Art glass
- Mid-Century Modern
- Fenton swung vase
- Retro
- Glass vase
- Mid Century
- Amber glass
- Bud vase
- Fenton glass
- Fenton vase
- Collectible glass
- Viking
- Amber
- Milk glass

Two things stand out to me in this list. One, *Mid-Century Modern* (MCM) appears three times, meaning it is a HOT keyword that you should use in your listing. Also, the list brought up several glass makers. Being able to identify the brand of glass vase you are selling will bring in more customers as the data shows that many people are searching for Fenton, LE Smith, and Viking.

PRO TIP: Use **Google Image Search** to help identify pieces you aren't sure about. Using my iPhone, I bring up *Google Images* and take a picture of the item in question. Usually, the results show numerous other pieces for sale, enabling me to identify not only the maker but also get more information about the item. The more information you can provide about the items you are selling, the more money you can command.

Back to our swung vase example. Let's say you can positively identify the vase as Fenton. A good title might be, *Vintage Fenton Blue Glass Swung Vase | Mid Century Modern MCM Home Décor Collectible | 9 Finger 11.5" Fenton Art Glass Vase*

I would then make sure to repeat the keywords used in the title in the description, which could read something like, *This stunning vintage Fenton blue glass swung vase has no chips or cracks. It features 9 'fingers and measures 11.5" from the base to the highest tip. It is perfect for anyone who loves mid-century modern home décor and collectibles.*

I would then add the most important keywords into the *Tags* section of the listing, which allows for 13 keywords:

1. Fenton
2. Mid-century modern
3. Swung vase
4. Vintage
5. MCM
6. Blue
7. Hand-painted
8. Swung glass vase
9. Midcentury modern
10. Mid-century vase
11. Blue swung vase
12. Fenton swung vase

13. 9 finger swung

To maximize your chances of getting discovered by potential customers, it's important to organize your listings into appropriate shop sections. For instance, using the vase example, you could create a dedicated section for *Fenton* and add all Fenton pieces to this section. By doing this, your Fenton items will be more easily discovered, and Etsy will also promote your other Fenton pieces when someone is looking at just one of your listings.

Since we've already repeated the term *Fenton* in the title, description, tags, and shop section, Etsy's algorithm will pick up on this keyword and show your listing to customers who search for *Fenton*. Additionally, Etsy will prioritize your Fenton listings when displaying ads on Google and social media platforms, further increasing your visibility to potential customers.

While you can repeat keywords in your titles, descriptions, and tags, you only get one shop section per item. Therefore, you want the shop section you add each item in to have the most relevant keyword. Using our Fenton vase example, *Fenton* is the most important keyword. Therefore, it makes for a good shop section. And since Fenton doesn't just make vases, it allows you to add all Fenton items into one section.]

Repeating keywords in your Etsy listings may feel tedious, but it's a necessary part of selling on the platform. Remember that you are competing with tens of thousands of other sellers who offer products similar to yours, so simply listing an item and hoping it will be found isn't enough. By using SEO techniques, you can ensure that your products appear in relevant search results. And after a while, it becomes easier and easier to figure out the best keywords on your own without having to do any research. These days I can list most items without using a third-party keyword search website.

Now that the SEO lecture is (once again!), out of the way, let's get to listing!

To create your first Etsy listing, log into your **Etsy Shop Manager**. Remember that your *Shop Manager* tab is easily located at the top of all your Etsy account pages; it's the little **shop icon**. After clicking on your *Shop Manager*, then click on the **Listings tab** on the left-hand side of the page. Then click on the **+ Add a listing** tab in the top right-hand corner of the page. This will bring up a blank listing template with the following fields to fill out:

Title: The *Title* section is one of the most important parts of your Etsy listing. It's the first thing customers will see when they're browsing through search results, so it needs to be descriptive and eye-catching. Etsy allows 140 characters in each title, and I recommend you use as many characters as possible to give your listing the best chance possible to be found in search results.

Good titles use descriptive words that accurately describe the item and use the most important keywords that customers might search for. Be sure to highlight any special features your item has. Avoid using all caps except for one or two of the most important words. Typing in all caps is considered "yelling" on the internet, so titles written in all caps have an off-putting effect on shoppers.

As another example of a good title, let's say you sell vintage jewelry and are listing a Lucite bracelet from the 1960s. A good title would be *Vintage Clear Lucite Women's Bracelet | Vintage Jewelry | Lucite | Mid Century Modern MCM 1960s Jewelry.*

You want to make sure the keywords you use in your titles are the ones customers are searching for. This is why a research tool such as EtsyCheck or eRank comes in handy, especially when you first start selling on Etsy. You just enter a few words about the item you are listing, and they will find the keywords that Etsy shoppers are using to find products like yours.

PRO TIP: If, when you are researching how to price an item, you come across sold listings, you can copy those titles to your own. Let's say you are listing a pair of Lucite candle sticks and you find several sold listings for sets that match the one you are listing. Copy the title of the set that brought in the most money. It has proven to be a winning title before, and it may be so again. Note, however, that you should only copy titles, not descriptions. And you cannot copy another seller's photos, as that is against Etsy's policies.

Photos: Adding at least one photo to your Etsy listing is mandatory. However, Etsy allows you to upload up to 10 photos per listing. Try to use all 10 slots if possible, as this gives potential customers a better sense of what your product looks like from different angles and perspectives. A good tip is to make sure your photos give the customer the same views as if they were holding the item in their own hands and turning it over to examine all sides.

The first photo in your listing, called the *thumbnail* photo, is the most important picture as it's the one that customers will see in search results and on the listing page. *Thumbnail* photos should measure 2000x2000 pixels. If you take a photo on your smartphone from within the Etsy listing, it should automatically size it for you.

Providing clear, well-lit, and visually appealing photos of your items is key to their selling. However, you don't need to have a professional photography set up; most sellers, including myself, take listing photos with an iPhone. Here are some tips for taking good Etsy listing photos:

1. **Use natural lighting:** Photograph your item in natural light, preferably near a window or outdoors. Add in lighting from lamps or ring lights as needed. Avoid using your camera's flash

as it can alter the actual color of the item.

2. **Use a plain background:** Choose a clean, simple background that won't distract from your item. A white or neutral-colored backdrop works well. I use white foam boards that I buy at dollar stores for most items, although I switch to black foam boards for colored glass.

3. **Get up close:** Take photos that show your item up close, so that potential customers can see the details and quality of your work. Make sure to photograph any brand markings, stickers, and flaws.

4. **Use a ruler:** While you will want to provide exact measurements in the description of your listing, you can show scale by using rulers or tape measurers in your photos. I use two large, clear rulers in my photos: One to measure the height and the other to measure the length.

5. **Avoid props:** It can be tempting to add props to make your items more appealing, but be careful as shoppers will assume that they are buying the prop, too. For instance, if you put flowers in a vase, most buyers will expect to see those flowers in the box when the vase arrives. Even if you put a disclaimer in the listing, most shoppers are notorious for not reading the descriptions. Save yourself the hassle and only photograph the item you are selling.

6. **Take multiple photos:** Take multiple photos from different angles to give shoppers a better sense of what your item actually looks like. Again, you want buyers to get the same views of the item as they would if there were holding it in their own hands.

7. **Edit your photos:** Use basic photo editing tools to adjust the brightness, contrast, and color balance of your photos if needed. Crop areas to zoom in on special details. You can accomplish most of these editing features within the Etsy

listing itself. However, save yourself time by trying to take the best photos possible the first time so you don't have to edit later on.

Video: In addition to photos, Etsy also allows you to include a 15-second video in each of your listings. While videos can be useful when selling crafts or handmade items, I personally don't advocate using them for antiques unless you are selling something extremely expensive. While I might consider taking a video clip of an $800 large LE Smith bittersweet swung vase, I wouldn't film a video for a $15 Lefton figurine.

Description: The *Description* section in an Etsy listing is where you provide more detailed information about your product and expand upon what you included in the title. Details you need to provide in the description include brands, measurements, colors, dates, and conditions. With antiques especially it is important that you only include information you know to be correct. For example, don't tell customers a vintage figurine was made in Japan if you do not know for sure. And don't guess about brands, either. If you aren't sure about a detail, then simply note that in the listing. It's better to omit a detail than put in something incorrect.

Note that online shoppers, including those on Etsy, are notorious for not reading listing descriptions and simply making purchases based on the photos. Making sure you include all of the details in your listing will protect you from cases where buyers claim their order didn't exactly match the photo or that the size wasn't what they expected. You will be able to point to your description and prove you did include all of the relevant information, regardless of whether or not the buyer read it.

Accurately describing the condition of your items is probably the most important detail you need to include when selling antiques on Etsy. Vintage items, even those still sealed in their original boxes, almost always have some wear to the packaging. China dishes may look pristine to the naked eye, but under light, you will often find scratches. Paint wear, torn stickers, and surface scuffs are common on older items. The majority of antique shoppers understand and expect items to show wear due to age, use, and storage; there is no need to try and fool them into thinking otherwise.

PRO TIP: The term *vintage patina* is common in the world of antiques and accounts for a number of condition issues, including rust and tarnishing.

I always under promise and over-deliver on condition, meaning if an item is in excellent condition, I will only describe it as in very good condition. I don't ever want a customer to have high expectations that may not be met when they receive their order. However, when I undervalue a piece, buyers are usually pleasantly surprised by its condition when they receive it, which is reflected in my feedback.

Finally, even though your shipping and return policies will be shown in a dedicated section of your listing, it's a good idea to include them in your listing descriptions. Again, the more places you can include details and policies, the better, as it will protect you from complaints after the sale.

While some sellers like to write their descriptions in paragraph form, I prefer using bullet points to highlight key information. Most customers aren't going to read a block of text, but they are likely to note the details when they simply stated. Here's an example of what a bullet point description might look like for the sample piece of jewelry we discussed earlier with the title: *Vintage Clear Lucite Women's Bracelet | Vintage Jewelry | Lucite | Mid Century Modern MCM 1960s Jewelry:*

- ***Vintage Women's Lucite Bracelet***
- ***From the estate of a 1960s Mid Century Modern jewelry***

collector
- *Faint scuffs on one section of the bracelet due to wear/ storage; please see photos for up close details.*
- *The clasp is intact and functioning with no rust*
- *We ship all orders within 3 business days*

Personalization: The personalization section of an Etsy listing allows you as a seller to provide custom options or personalization for your customers. Most antique sellers do not offer personalization, so you can simply remove this option.

Price: It's now time to price your item! If you have been selling your antiques in a booth or at shows, you may need to make some adjustments to pricing them on Etsy. In many instances, you will likely be able to charge more for your antiques on Etsy than you can at in-person events. When you sell on Etsy, you are selling to a global market. While you often can't charge full retail price locally (unless you want to wait years for the right buyer to come along), on Etsy it is expected that vintage collectibles are priced at full retail value.

However, note that condition is a major factor in how much you can charge for vintage collectibles. A mistake I see many antique dealers make is that they put a full retail price on their items despite the condition. Full retail price means the piece needs to be in pristine condition. Every chip, crack, color fade, or spot of crazing devalues your piece. A vintage collectible in its original box will command more than one without the box. A piece of glass with the original sticker still attached will sell for more than a piece without.

So how do you know how to price your items? The first thing you want to do is search Etsy for the item you are selling to see if anyone else is selling what you are listing. Chances are, you will find several other shops with the same item you have. Take a look at not only their pricing but also the condition of the item to get an idea of what you may be able to charge for yours.

I also recommend going over to **eBay** and doing a completed listing search for the item you are listing. While Etsy doesn't have a way to filter sold listings, eBay does. Search for the item you are selling on eBay and then, if you are on a desktop computer, look on the left-hand side of the screen and scroll down until you find a section titled **Show Only.** Here you can select both **Completed Listings** and **Sold Listings.** The *Sold Listings* option will only show you the items that sold, but the *Completed Listings* option will also show you the listings that didn't sell. By studying why some listings sold while others didn't, you will be able to figure out how much you can realistically charge for your item.

If you can't find the item you are selling on Etsy or eBay, try using *Google Image Search* at images.google.com. If you are using a desktop computer, you can upload a photo to the site; if you are on your smartphone, you can take the picture right from your phone. Google will then search the internet using your image, trying to match it to listings on Etsy, eBay, and other websites. The vast majority of the time, a *Google Image Search* will lead you to a listing that will help you in identifying and pricing your piece.

PRO TIP: My go-to website for researching antiques and collectibles is **Replacements.com,** which is a website that specializes in vintage items, and I use the site to research China dishes, silverware, glass, figurines, and collectibles. Not only am I often able to get more details about a particular item, but I can see what the item sells for in various conditions.

Etsy Fee Calculator: Finally, before deciding on a price, I recommend using an Etsy fee calculator so you will know exactly how much you will make on an item after the cost of goods, fees, and shipping. I use

omniprofitcalculator.com/etsy-fee-calculator, but there are other free calculators online that you can use.

As an example, let's say your purchase a vintage Hummel figurine for $5. Through research, you see that, in the condition yours is in, it sells for around $30. It will also cost $5 to ship the item. You decide to build the cost of shipping into the item so that it will be "free" for the customer. However, the cost of shipping will come out of the sale price.

An Etsy calculator will tell you that you would make $16.70 on the sale of the figurine. However, if you decided to charge the customer shipping, your profit would increase to $21.23. Remember, however, that there are other costs you will have to account for, such as mileage on your vehicle, shipping supplies, and, of course, taxes.

PRO TIP: Etsy pushes for sellers to opt into their *free shipping on orders of $35 or more* promise. If you sell lower-dollar items, opting into this program may lead to higher order totals as customers may add more to their shopping carts to hit the $35 threshold.

PRO TIP: Even if you offer free shipping on all of your products, still opt into Etsy's $35 free shipping promotion as they will add your shop to the program. Your shop will receive priority in search results alongside other shops that offer the guarantee, even though your customers receive free shipping, anyway.

Quantity: The *Quantity* section of an Etsy listing allows you to specify how many of a particular item you have available for sale. When selling antiques, you will likely only have one of each item you are listing. However, if you do have multiples, it is very important that you only list them within the same listing if they are in the exact same condition.

For example, let's say you have two identical vintage owl brooches. However, one brooch has a bit of paint wear on the front, while the other does not. You do not want to list these brooches in the same listings. Instead, you would want to create two separate listings, noting the condition differences in each.

However, let's say you have four sets of vintage Hallmark coffee mugs that are in the same condition with no chips, cracks, spoon marks, or paint wear. As long as each mug is exactly the same, you could list these in the same listing with a quantity of four.

Category: The *Category* section of an Etsy listing allows you to select the most relevant category for your item, which in turn will help shoppers find you. Etsy will usually offer you suggestions based on your title, but you can override those options by typing in your product into the search bar to see what comes up. If you aren't sure which category to choose from the results, try searching on Etsy to see which categories sellers of similar items are listing their products in.

Most categories on Etsy have subcategories. The great thing about this is that Etsy will automatically put your listing in both the main category and any relevant subcategories, which increases the chance of your item being found in the search. Select as many subcategories as Etsy offers you to widen your net on the site.

Tags: The *Tags* section of an Etsy listing is where you can add relevant keywords that describe your item. *Tags* help customers to find your item when they search for those specific keywords on Etsy. As previously mentioned, *Tags* are a part of Etsy SEO. You want to repeat relevant keywords in your *Title, Description, Shop Section,* and *Tags* to give them the best chance of being found in search.

As I've already mentioned, I use both eRank and EtsyCheck to search for the best *Tags* for my listings. Sites such as these give me the keywords that Etsy shoppers are typing into search and also show me which keywords lead to sales.

Etsy allows you to add up to 13 *Tags* for each item. Be sure to use all of the available tags to maximize your item's visibility in search results. I like to use a mix of the most popular keywords along with some that are lower in rank to spread my reach as wide as possible. Because Etsy is such a competitive marketplace, using a handful of less relevant keywords can help reach more customers.

Materials: While some Etsy categories have a listing section where you can choose materials from a drop-down menu, the options in these menus can be limited. Fortunately, there is another section in the listing template where you can manually enter the material of the item you are selling. Even if you noted the material in the listing description, it is still helpful to add it again here as it can better help the chance of your item being shown to customers searching for that material.

Shipping: Well, we've reached the section of the listing that most new online sellers fear. Shipping. I devote an entire chapter to shipping on Etsy in the next chapter of this book. But for now, here's a quick step-by-step instruction list:

1. To accurately calculate shipping costs, you will need a digital postage scale to weigh packages for shipment. These can be found for under $20 on Amazon.
2. Weigh the item you are listing inside of a shipping box. It doesn't have to be the box you end up using to ship the product, but you want a similar size box to get an estimated weight. You also want to add a few ounces to account for the weight of packing materials.
3. If the package measures over .25" in depth and/or weighs 4 ounces or more, you can choose to ship via USPS Ground or Priority Mail. Postcards, stamps, and other ephemera that can fit into a standard-size envelope and measure less than .25" in depth can be sent via USPS First Class Mail.

4. Unless you are selling ephemera, you will most likely be shipping items that will need to ship via Ground or Priority.

5. Ground is generally the most cost-effective option for heavier packages, but Priority is faster and sometimes may cost the same or even less than Ground. Priority also provides additional shipping options such as insurance along with FREE shipping boxes.

6. You only need to enter the shipping range, not the exact ounces, to ship via Ground or Priority. Under one pound, one to two pounds, two to three pounds, three to four pounds, etc.

7. If you are shipping via First Class Mail (i.e. in a standard-size mailing envelope), you will need to enter the ounces as one, two, or three. Envelopes weighing four ounces or more will ship via Ground or Priority.

8. Enter the package weight when listing the item on Etsy. This will allow Etsy to present you with the available shipping options.

9. Select the shipping option(s) you want to offer customers. Consider offering multiple shipping options to accommodate customers with different needs and budgets. For example, you may offer Ground as the first option but offer Priority as the second. I frequently offer Ground as a "FREE" option but give customers the choice to pay for Priority.

10. When a customer places an order, Etsy will calculate the postage based on the weight you entered and the shipping option they selected. The cost will also depend on the distance between you and your customer. If you are in Florida and shipping to a customer in Florida, the cost will be less than if you are shipping to a customer in California.

11. Once Etsy has determined the cost of postage, you can purchase and print the shipping label through Etsy. The cost

of the label will be deducted from your balance.

12. Because you printed the label through Etsy, the tracking number will immediately be loaded to both your and your customer's accounts. This allows you and the customer to track the package during shipping and lets you know when the package arrives.

13. You can also print out a packing slip during this process to include with the order.

Returns & Exchanges: Most sellers of antiques do not allow for returns or exchanges unless they made a mistake in accurately describing the product. However, this is only a decision you can make. Note that if you made an error when you listed the item, it's easier to issue the customer a full refund and allow them to keep the product rather than ask them to ship the product back to you and pay for the return shipping. Or, if it was a minor mistake, you can offer them a partial refund. Many times a customer actually wants to keep the item but also wants some compensation for the error on your part.

Shop Section: As we've already discussed, *Shop Sections* are your Etsy store categories. Remember that you want to make sure your listing titles match your shop sections to maximize Etsy SEO. You can have 20 sections in your shop, and you can edit them at any time.

Renewal Options: When you list an item for sale on Etsy, you have the option to choose between *Manual Renewal* and *Automatic Renewal.* *Manual Renewal* means that after four months, Etsy will end your listing. You will then need to manually renew it. With *Automatic Renewal,* Etsy will automatically renew the listing every four months. It costs $.20 to list an item for four months on Etsy; with automatic renewal, you agree to be charged another $.20 when Etsy renews the listing.

I always recommend that when you first list an item you choose *Manual Renewal* as it allows you to reevaluate the listing after four months and make any necessary edits or adjustments. This allows you to see how your listing is performing and make changes to improve it. For instance, you may realize you need to add more pictures or that you need to adjust the price.

However, if after another four months, the item hasn't sold, you should decide whether or not to keep it in your store. Some sellers turn automatic renewal on and let items sit in their shops for years. Others pull items if they don't sell after some time. How long to leave an item listed is a decision only you can make.

Publish: Once you have filled out the listing form and have doubled checked to make sure everything is correct, you simply click on the *Publish* button, which will make the listing live on Etsy's site. Your item is now available for sale on Etsy! Note that you can edit the listing even after it has gone live.

Listing Your Second Item: Once you have published your first listing, it's time to tackle the second. However, instead of starting from scratch by clicking on the + *Add a listing* button, you can use the *sell similar* method of simply making a **Copy** of an existing listing and changing the item specifics. It works particularly well if you are listing similar items back-to-back, such as vintage Christmas ornaments or antique glass as you will only have to change out certain details. The *Copy* option is found on the photo of each listing; just **click on the little screw icon** to bring it up.

Just Keep Listing: Note that it takes a while to build a successful Etsy shop. It's hard to get people to buy from you when you only have a few items listed. The fact is that the most successful Etsy shops have hundreds and sometimes thousands of active listings. The more items you list for sale, the better your chances of making sales. Don't let a lack of sales get you down. Just keep on listing!

PRO TIP: Retail has its slow times and its busy times. Summer is typically a slow sales period as kids are out of school and families take vacations. The busiest times for antique sellers are typically fourth quarter (October through December when people are holiday shopping) and first quarter (January through March when people are stuck inside for the winter and shopping online). I prepare for the slow times by putting money aside during the busy sales months. That way I have money to source and to load my shop up during the summer in order to be ready for the busy Christmas shopping season. I always say that spring and summer are for sourcing, while fall and winter are for selling!

CHAPTER SEVEN: ETSY SHIPPING MADE EASY

The time has come: You've made your first Etsy sale! It's okay to do a little happy dance, you've earned it!

Note that you can enable notifications on your smartphone through the Etsy app so that you will get an alert every time an order comes in. Otherwise, you need to make a point to check your *Seller Dashboard* at least twice daily to see if you have any new orders. But regardless of how you check your account, there is an order awaiting shipment!

FUN FACT: If you enable notifications, you will hear a cash register sound every time you make a sale! There's nothing better than hearing that CHA-CHING sound as it means you are making money!

However, once a sale has come through, a new job starts as you will need to ship out the order. But before you can package an order, you need shipping supplies. Because antiques come in all shapes and sizes, what shipping supplies you need will vary based on what you sell. If you sell jewelry, you may want to invest in cardboard jewelry boxes with cushioned inserts (you can buy these in bulk on Amazon). If you sell ephemera, you may want to purchase cardboard mailers to ensure orders aren't bent during the shipping process. And if you are shipping larger items, you will need shipping boxes. Many antique sellers such as myself sell a wide variety of items and therefore keep a wide variety of shipping boxes on hand for all items.

But boxes are just the start of the shipping supplies you will need to sell antiques on Etsy. Here is what most Etsy vintage sellers keep on hand for their businesses:

Digital Postage Scale: As we discussed earlier in this book, you will need to have a digital postal scale to weigh packages to figure out the correct postage. You can buy digital scales for around $20 to $30 on Amazon, and they are also sold at office supply stores. Look for a "postage/mail" specific scale that measures pounds AND ounces, as you will need to know ounces when shipping items under one pound or at the mail rate.

Some sellers who sell items that are all similar in size, such as jewelry, coins, postcards, or ephemera, choose to charge a flat rate for all their orders. For example, many jewelry sellers charge $5 to ship any of their items as everything they sell weighs under one pound. In other cases, sellers offer "free" shipping on all orders as they build the shipping cost into their price. One seller may charge $5 to ship a $30 vintage necklace while another seller may sell a similar piece for $35 with "free" shipping.

Shipping, of course, is never free. Someone has to pay for postage, whether you charge the customer or pay for it out of your balance. This is where an Etsy fee calculator, as we discussed earlier in this book, comes in very handy. Again, my favorite can be found at omniprofitcalculator.com/etsy-fee-calculator/.

If you sell items that weigh over one pound, you will want to let Etsy calculate the shipping cost for both you and your customer based on the weight of the package and the distance between your two zip codes. This method ensures that the customer pays the exact postage needed for you to ship them their order.

Some sellers offer "free" shipping, padding the item's cost into their estimated shipping charge. While offering "free" shipping can be a smart move for lightweight items that weigh under one pound, it can backfire on heavier items as buyers know when a seller has inflated the price of an item to cover shipping.

For example, if you are selling a piece of vintage pottery that weighs over five pounds when it is packaged for shipment, it will be hard to add the $15 shipping cost to the price. Most customers understand that heavy items cost more to ship and, if they want an item, they will pay the cost. However, if you add the shipping to the price of the item, you may lose that customer as they will see another seller's price is lower than yours.

Printer & Labels: There are a few different options for addressing and posting your Etsy orders. The first is to simply print labels onto paper, cut them out, and tape them to boxes. People laugh when I tell them I used this method for many years, but I did! At the time, it was cost-effective and worked just fine for my business model. You can certainly start by using this method, especially if you are completely new to shipping and just want to get used to the process. Don't let more experienced sellers shame you about it, either!

These days, however, using a shipping label printer is arguably the most efficient way to print shipping labels. On Etsy, you can purchase and print shipping labels directly from the platform. This will save you time compared to handwriting addresses or taking orders to the post office. When a customer buys an item from you on Etsy, their shipping address is immediately added to a label. Etsy calculates the postage based on the weight of the item the distance it will travel; and when you print the shipping label, the cost is deducted from your balance. You do not have to type in addresses, research postage rates, or pay an invoice at the end of the month. It is all done automatically, which makes it so easy!

To print shipping labels from Etsy, you'll need a printer that is compatible with the labels you are using. There are two different types of printers that you can use:

Thermal Printer: This type of printer doesn't use ink, but it does require special labels. It's a good option if you want to avoid the hassle of replacing ink cartridges or toner. A thermal printer works by using heat to transfer inkless media onto paper. It consists of a print head with a row of tiny heating elements that are activated according to the digital image of the document being printed. When the heating elements are activated, they cause a thermal reaction in the inkless media, which results in the transfer of the media onto the paper.

I use a Rollo thermal printer specifically for printing my Etsy sticker shop order labels. While I do not have to purchase ink for the printer, I do have to buy special labels. It's a small machine that sits right next to my computer, making it easy to print, peel, and stick labels to envelopes.

LaserJet Printer: This type of printer uses toner to print, and it can be a good option for printing shipping labels as well as packing slips for larger orders. LaserJet printers are known for their speed, reliability, and high-quality printing as well as their affordable pricing. They can print on a wide range of media, including envelopes, labels, and cardstock.

LaserJet printers are more efficient and cost-effective than inkjet printers when it comes to printing large volumes of documents. However, they do require toner, which can be more expensive than ink in the long run. I use a thermal printer to print shipping labels but use my LaserJet printer to print packing slips for larger Etsy orders. However, I do sometimes use label sheets in my LaserJet printer; these sheets print two peel-and-stick labels per page.

Freebies: Including free items in orders is a common practice among Etsy shops. This can be a nice way to show appreciation to your customers and promote your business. Stickers or magnets with your URL or brand name are the most popular freebies as they offer an affordable way for you to promote your business and encourage customers to visit your shop or website. I use StickerMule to print my enclosure stickers. I have a wide variety of both stickers and magnets with my website URL printed on them.

Some sellers add freebies that coordinate with the items they sell. This is more common with craft sellers. For example, candle makers may include a book of matches with orders. Freebies aren't a requirement for any Etsy shop. You don't want freebies to add to the weight of your package, and you don't want to invest money into items that will only be thrown away. Most customers are happy with well packaged items that arrive quickly and don't care about free gifts.

Boxes & Envelopes: You cannot just stick a shipping label directly onto an antique and stick it in the mailbox. Shipping packages require *shipping supplies*, and that means shipping boxes and envelopes, such as:

- **Plain cardboard shipping boxes in various sizes**
- **USPS Priority shipping boxes**
- **Poly mailers**
- **Bubble mailers**
- **Cardboard envelope mailers**

The United States Postal Service (USPS) is the best resource for small businesses because they offer FREE *Priority Mail* shipping boxes. While *Priority Mail* is an excellent option for shipping many packages, you will need other forms of packaging if you sell items that qualify for *Media Mail* and *Ground,* as well as for international shipments (again, more on these forms of shipping coming up). Basically, you need two forms of shipping boxes/envelopes: *Priority Mail* boxes and envelopes, and plain boxes and envelopes for the rest.

Visit (and bookmark!) store.usps.com/store/results/shipping-supplies/_/N-7d0v8v?_requestid=217274 for all of the free supplies the Post Office offers.

USPS Standard Priority Boxes: The sizes of boxes you will need depends on what you sell. You can order *Priority Mail* boxes for free online; your mail carrier will deliver them to your door. Here are the most popular box sizes:

- **Priority Mail Show Box SHOEBOX:** 14-7/8 x 7-3/8 x 5.24 (not just for shoes, but for anything long and narrow)
- **Priority Mail Box 1097 Rectangle:** 11-5/8 x 2.5x 13-7/16
- **Priority Mail Box 1905 Rectangle:** 12.5 x 3-1/8 x 15-5/8
- **Priority Mail Box 1092 Rectangle:** 12.25 x 2-7/8 x 13-11/16
- **Priority Mail Box 1096L Rectangle:** 9-7/16 x 6-7/16 x 2-3/16
- **Large Priority Mail Box 7:** 12.25 x 12 x 8.5 (largest size of the Priority Mail boxes; perfect for shipping larger products or several smaller items in one box)
- **Priority Mail Box 4:** 7.25 x 7.25 x 6.25 (square size is perfect for shipping mugs, figurines, and small, rounded items)
- **Priority Mail Padded Flat Rate Envelope:** 9.5 x 12.5 (the go-to choice for shipping heavy sets of flatware, flat metal objects, and anything that you can stuff inside that isn't prone to breakage)

In addition to the FREE *Priority Mail* boxes, you can also order FREE **USPS Priority Stickers,** which are perfect for covering writing on the outside of repurposed boxes. There are two options to choose from:

- **Priority Mail Sticker Label Roll of 1000**

- **Priority Mail Shipping Label of 10**

When you look through all the available choices for *Priority Mail* boxes and envelopes, you will see that USPS offers many other options that I did not list above, including *Flat Rate* and *Express* boxes. As you continue along your Etsy journey, you will learn which shipping boxes and envelopes you use the most, and therefore, which you need to reorder frequently. You'll also know if you want to branch out into *Flat Rate* or *Express* packaging. The vast majority of Etsy sellers, however, stick to the regular *Priority Mail* options.

The Post Office offers these free shipping supplies in quantities as low as ten each. Depending on the sizes of products you sell, you may want to order some of each just to have them on hand. However, I find that I mostly use Box 7, Box 4, and the Padded Flat Rate Envelopes the most, although I do keep a small supply of the rectangle boxes on hand as well as the "shoe boxes", which are great for longer items such as dolls that are too thick to fit in the rectangle boxes.

Note that sometimes it can take quite a while for *Priority Mail* boxes to be delivered due to supply issues, so do not wait until you are completely out to order more, especially heading into the busy holiday season. I order my supply of *Priority Mail* boxes in September in anticipation of the fourth quarter. While some Post Office locations keep a supply in stock, many do not. My location has to order boxes the same way I do to stock their retail section!

While *Priority Mail* is an excellent option for shipping most packages, you will need other forms of packaging for **Media Mail** (if you sell books) and **Ground Advantage** (for boxes too heavy to ship via Priority), as those methods of postage can NOT be mailed in the *Priority Mail* boxes. It is against USPS policy to alter the *Priority* boxes in any way, so forget thinking you can turn them inside out (they are printed with *Priority Mail* on the inside to thwart this) or put stickers on the outside to conceal the fact that they are indeed *Priority*. Misusing USPS supplies can result in your losing your postal account.

Before you run out and buy new shipping boxes and envelopes, however, check around your house to see what you have on hand. Plain cardboard boxes, manila envelopes, and bubble mailers can all be used for non-priority mail as long as they are in good, clean condition. While eBay sellers can get away with patching up beat-up boxes, Etsy sellers cannot as Etsy customers have higher expectations in not only the items they buy but in how they are delivered. I save every strong, clean shipping box I receive as well as good packing materials to reuse in my online businesses.

Take an inventory of the various sizes of your current antiques to determine the packaging you will need. Perhaps you will only sell glass, for which poly and bubble mailers are not needed. On the other hand, if you only sell ephemera, you may not need to worry about stocking up on large boxes.

I sell different types of products on several different platforms, so I keep a wide variety of boxes and envelopes in my shipping supply area. While I utilize the free *Priority Mail* boxes and bubble mailers from the Post Office, I also invest in plain shipping boxes from Amazon, eBay, Uline, and Value Mailers for *Media* and *Ground* packages. And I have bubble mailer envelopes that I buy at Sam's Club and poly mailers that I order on Amazon.

For my online businesses, I keep the following plain boxes and envelopes on hand:

- **Plain Cardboard Shipping Boxes** (4", 6", 8", 10", and 12" sizes)
- **Oversized Cardboard Shipping Boxes** (14" and 16" sizes for when I have to ship oversized items via Parcel or UPS)

- **Poly Mailers in various sizes** (for shipping textiles and plush)
- **Bubble Mailers in various sizes** (for items that need more cushioning than a plain poly mailer)
- **Cardboard Mailers in various sizes** (for shipping ephemera that I do not want to bend in the mail)

Packing Materials: You cannot just throw an item into a box and ship it with no packing materials to buffer it inside the box (well, you CAN, as I have seen many sellers do, but you should not). You need to WRAP up your items to protect them inside the box. You want to ensure that the item is protected from being thrown around, inside planes and trucks, and tossed onto customers' porches. Depending on what you sell and how much protection your products need, these are supplies you may want to consider:

- **Recycled Packing Paper** (to wrap up items inside of the shipping box)
- **Bubble Wrap** (essential for protecting breakables)
- **Packing Peanuts** (perfect for buffering breakables inside of boxes)
- **Shipping Tape** (buy the largest rolls and the strongest type you can)
- **Tissue Paper** (better than packing paper for wrapping delicate breakables)
- **Cardboard Corrugated Rolls** (allows you to create a box-in-a-box around breakables)

Shipping Tape: You now have an assortment of boxes, envelopes, packing paper, newspaper, bubble wrap, packing peanuts, cardboard rolls, and/or tissue paper to protect your items during shipping. To seal your packages, you need shipping tape.

Note that you want to purchase *SHIPPING tape,* not packing tape. Packing tape is for moving boxes and is not as strong, while shipping tape is meant to hold packages together as they travel to their destination by vehicle, boat, and/or air.

Most sellers use a **handheld tape dispenser** (usually sold right next to the tape at stores) when sealing their packages. If you are just starting out selling on Etsy, I recommend buying a kit with the tape dispenser included along with extra rolls of tape. You can usually find such kits for $10 to $15 in the tape section of the big box stores. You only need to buy the dispenser once and then just buy tape refills as needed. Throughout the year, the shipping tape at Sam's Club and Costco goes on sale; when it does, I stock up. These warehouse clubs offer the best deals on shipping tape. If you don't have a location near you, you can order from both online.

Now for the most confusing part of selling on Etsy for new sellers: **Shipping!**

There are dozens of carriers and ways you can ship packages. While UPS and FedEx are viable shipping options, you will want to stick with shipping your packages through the United States Postal Service (USPS) when you are just starting your online business. The USPS provides the best value and service for small sellers, and Etsy has partnered with them to make shipping easy and cost-effective. Since the USPS is Etsy's preferred shipping partner, if you sell on Etsy, you will be using them a lot.

While there are numerous ways you can ship a package through the Post Office, most Etsy sellers ship via one of four methods, all of which are for shipments within the United States (including San Juan, Puerto Rico, and military bases):

- **Media Mail**

- **First Class Mail**
- **Ground Advantage**
- **Priority Mail**

Media Mail: Media Mail is for, surprise, MEDIA! It is preferable to ship books via *Media Mail* because they are heavy, and you get a discounted rate. However, the low price also means that *Media Mail* is extremely slow, sometimes taking up to one month (although the Post Office claims delivery is two to eight business days).

The following items qualify to be shipped via *Media Mail*:

- **Books of at least eight printed pages**
- **16-millimeter or narrower-width films and catalogs of films 24 pages or more**
- **Printed music**
- **Educational testing materials and printed educational materials**
- **Sound recordings**
- **Playscripts and manuscripts**
- **Loose-leaf pages and their binders of education medical information**
- **Computer-readable media**

Media Mail can NOT be used for current advertising, video games, computer drives, or digital drives. The maximum weight for a *Media Mail* package is 70 pounds.

Some sellers try to cheat the system by shipping heavy, non-media items via *Media Mail*. This is a violation of the USPS policy and can result in you losing your postal account. Post offices are notorious for opening boxes marked as *Media Mail* to ensure they only contain approved media items, so be careful to follow the rules.

Media Mail **items can only be shipped in plain boxes or envelopes**, NOT in *Priority Mail* boxes. When you print a label via Etsy (more on how to do this coming up), it will clearly state on the label which service you paid for. So, if you print a *Media Mail* label, it will say "MEDIA MAIL" at the top.

First Class Mail: *First Class Mail* is the service you use when you send a postcard or letter weighing 3.5 ounces or less. While one stamp equals one ounce on a rectangular postcard or letter up to 3.5 ounces, anything 4 ounces or larger is charged at a higher package. Unless you are selling flat lightweight items that fit in letter envelopes, you will be paying the package rate to ship your Etsy orders. Note that any envelope more than .25" in depth has to ship via a package rate. Things like coins or stacks of postcards are often too thick to be sent via *First Class Mail*.

Ground Advantage: *Ground Advantage* (formerly called *Parcel Post*) is for packages weighing over 4 ounces and/or over .25" in depth. *Ground* is a bit slower than *Priority*, but it is cheaper for heavy items. **Ground shipments must be in plain boxes or envelopes**; just as with *Media Mail*, you can NOT ship *Ground* shipments in the *Priority Mail* boxes. The maximum weight for *Ground* packages is 70 pounds.

Ground postage cost depends on the weight of the package and where it is going. That is why it is wise to use Etsy's *Calculated Shipping* as the customer pays for the exact shipping for their zip code.

While *Ground* is an excellent option for heavy packages, you want to make sure to check the cost between *Ground* and *Priority* when you are creating your shipping label through Etsy (again, I will be going over how to do this coming up). Depending on how far away the package is going, *Priority Mail* may be the cheaper option.

For example, I am in Iowa, centrally located on both coasts in the middle of the country. For packages weighing less than four pounds, it is often cheaper for me to ship via *Priority Mail* over *Ground*. Plus, I get to use a free *Priority Mail* shipping box.

What is great about shipping through Etsy is you can look at all the package and price options before paying for and printing a label. That way, you can find the best rate AND fastest shipping time for each order. It is always nice when a customer pays for *Ground,* but you can upgrade them to *Priority*. Not only do you save money by being able to use a free Priority box, but the item arrives much faster, which always makes customers happy.

Priority Mail: *Priority Mail* is for packages that need to get to their location quickly, typically in 2-3 business days. Note that "business days" means weekdays and does not include Saturdays, Sundays, or federal holidays. If you ship an item out on a Friday, realize that it may not be processed and scanned at your area Post Office until Monday. From there, it will have an additional two to three days before it reaches the customer.

As I explained above when discussing *Ground Advantage*, sometimes *Priority Mail* can be the cheaper option. For me, this is often true for packages weighing less than four pounds that go as far as the West or East coasts. In fact, most of my shipments go via *Priority Mail* as nine times out of ten, it ends up being the cheapest option for packages between one and four pounds. And I save money as I can use a free *Priority* box rather than a plain cardboard box I had to purchase.

In addition to the faster shipping time, the best thing about *Priority Mail* is the FREE boxes. With the rising cost of supplies, a free box is always preferable over purchasing one. Single shipping boxes at Walmart cost over a dollar and get more expensive the larger the size. There are many sizes of *Priority Mail* boxes, some of which we've already discussed, including *Flat Rate* options. While the Post Office promotes their *Flat Rate* boxes as having the best postage costs, regular *Priority Mail* is usually cheaper for packages less than four pounds. Why? Because remember, when it comes to *Priority Mail,* it is not just the weight of the box but also the distance a package has to travel.

As I mentioned previously, I live in Iowa. I can send a two-pound package to Minnesota for a little over $7. However, that same package costs over $12 to ship to California. If that package goes to New York, the postage is around $11. To Hawaii or Alaska, the cost jumps to $15. Again, it is not just the weight but the distance the package must travel.

The type of *Priority Mail* box (*Regular or Flat Rate*) does not affect the speed of delivery. *Priority* is *Priority.* The difference in the shipping cost depends on the type and size of the box.

When packages are sorted for shipment at the Post Office, the most expensive postage options go first as they are guaranteed space on the trucks and planes. *Overnight* and *Express* are the most expensive since customers pay for one-to-two-day delivery. Next comes *Priority,* followed by *Ground. Media Mail* and *Bulk Mail* (bulk mail is usually "junk" mail that is sent out in mass) are the cheapest and, therefore, the last packages to be put out for delivery. It is all about available space; the more room on the truck or plane, the more packages they will ship out. is always in your best interest as a seller to use the fastest option available, even if you pay some change out of pocket. The faster the customer receives their order, the happier they will be!

The Post Office promotes *Priority Mail* as being delivered in two to three business days. Again, that is BUSINESS days, i.e., WEEKDAYS. While some large postal facilities process mail on the weekends, the vast majority do not. Mail and packages are not processed on federal holidays, either. Etsy stands behind sellers in shipping times when it comes to mailing out orders on weekends and holidays; keep these rules in mind if you have a customer demanding that the order they placed on Friday arrive by Monday. Etsy will also protect sellers in case of a major weather event or disaster for sellers in affected areas.

PRO TIP: Since the Post Office has eliminated *First Class PACKAGE* and replaced it, along with *Parcel Select,* with *Ground Advantage*, I no longer worry about getting the exact ounces for packages under one pound. With *First Class Package,* the ounces mattered. With *Ground Advantage*, the price difference between a four-ounce package and an eight-ounce package is so minimal that it isn't worth stressing over. I now look at all packages in the pound ranges: under one pound, one to two pounds, two to three pounds, etc.

International Shipping: International shipping used to be such a massive headache that most online sellers avoided it altogether. While you certainly do not need to ship to Canada, South America, or overseas, doing so will significantly increase your business. Fortunately, these days Etsy makes shipping international orders easy.

Gone are the days when sellers had to fill out lengthy customs forms by hand. Now when you choose your domestic shipping options in an Etsy listing, you can also choose other countries you will ship orders to. Etsy will calculate the cost for the buyer, and the label you print will have the customs form information right on it. You simply put the label onto the package just as you would for a domestic order and the Post Office will handle the delivery. So easy!

One negative aspect of shipping internationally is that international packages' tracking varies greatly and is quite unreliable. While Canada, the United Kingdom, and Australia all offer easy-to-track, generally reliable shipments, there are some areas of the world you may want to consider avoiding. I have been selling online since 2005 and have shipped to every corner of the globe. That being said, these days I avoid shipping packages to Central and South America, Africa, the Middle East, and Italy.

While the other European countries offer fairly reliable shipping, Italy is notorious for holding packages up in customs and losing them. Mexico along with Central and South American counties also have poor tracking, and shipping anywhere in Africa or the Middle East is risky as many online scams originate from those regions. Most international customers who buy from American Etsy sellers are in Canada, England, and Australia; and many sellers only sell to these countries.

PRO TIP: If you are nervous about international shipping, try offering it just to Canada to start with. Canada and the United States have an effective, reliable system for mail passing between the two countries. Many Canadian buyers shop on Etsy's U.S. site and understand the shipping costs and longer delivery times. And since Canadians speak English, even those who live in French-speaking areas, communicating with buyers is easy.

Once a shipment arrives in the buyer's country, it must first go through customs. As I have mentioned, some countries do this very quickly, while others (sorry Italy, but I'm pointing at you) are notoriously slow. International shipping can take as little as a week to arrive in Canada or up to a month or more for countries overseas. Fortunately, when you print shipping labels through Etsy, they protect against lost or stolen packages as well as for delivery delays. This is just one more reason why it is important to buy and print your labels directly through your Etsy account and not on third-party sites.

How To Set Up Shipping In Your Listings: Within the Etsy listing form, the shipping settings are located under **SHIPPING.**

Under **Shipping,** there is a box titled **Shipping option.** Click on **Select profile.** Then click **+ Create new profile** and edit the following fields:

Shipping Prices: Choose **Calculate them for me**

Origin ZIP code: Enter the zip code you will be shipping packages from

Processing Time: Enter how long it will take you to prepare, package, and put the package in the mail. Choose the fastest processing time you can as fast shipping will help you attract more buyers. I have my setting at 2-3 business days, but I usually ship the following business day. If you are completely new to selling online, I would recommend entering a three-day handling time so you can get used to shipping out orders. However, as soon as you are comfortable shortening that time, do so as it gives you an advantage over your competitors.

Where I'll ship: Here you can select the countries and regions you will ship to. We've already discussed the pros and cons of shipping internationally. You can start by only shipping within your own country if that feels the most comfortable to you and expand to shipping internationally once you have more experience.

Shipping Services: Etsy automatically selects all options available, so you will need to deselect the ones you don't want. For flat envelopes weighing under 4 ounces, choose *USPS First Class Mail.* For anything weighing over 4 ounces, choose either *Ground Advantage, Priority Mail,* or both. Offering both will allow the buyer to choose which they prefer.

If you offer international shipping, select *Standard International.* Note that *Media Mail is* located under the *Advanced shipping services* tab.

Free Shipping: Etsy is a big proponent of offering "free" shipping, even offering to boost your listings if you at least offer "free" shipping on orders of $35 or more. However, as noted earlier, "free" shipping can get you into trouble if you aren't properly building the postage cost into the price of your items. I only offer "free" shipping on lightweight items. And even in those cases I only offer *Free domestic shipping*; I do not offer *Free international shipping*. The cost of international postage is simply too high for sellers to absorb. I charge buyers shipping on all orders over one pound as well as all international orders.

Depending on what you sell, you may be able to adjust your prices to meet the "free" shipping for orders of $35 or more. But don't bend to the pressure to offer "free" shipping if the costs are too much to absorb. If you sell larger items, it will be nearly impossible to build the cost of shipping into the price of your item, and that's okay. Most customers often expect items like jewelry and stationary to ship for "free," but they usually understand that they will need to pay the shipping costs for heavy pottery pieces and fragile glass vases.

Check out what your competition is doing for their shipping. If everyone who is selling a similar Item you are listing is charging the customer shipping, then you won't have to worry about losing customers to another shop simply because of shipping charges. But if the majority of listings similar to yours are offering "free" shipping, it will be hard to attract buyers if you don't, too.

Handling Fee: Etsy allows sellers to charge buyers a handling fee. However, this is something I avoid. With the rising supply costs and postage rates, it's hard enough to price items competitively. Adding a handling charge will only push your prices higher, which can turn off potential shoppers. I recommend adding your packing costs to the price of your item as much as possible.

Item Weight & Size: Once you've finished filling out the *Shipping* options section, you will next need to enter the weight and size of the package.

When you are dealing with weights over four ounces or depths over .25" (remember, flat envelopes that weigh one, two, or three ounces can ship via First Class Mail), you do NOT need to know the EXACT weight; you only need to know the RANGE between pounds. Understanding that you only need to know the RANGE will make your shipping process go much more smoothly.

Here's the Trick: If you know the item you are selling will ship within the one-to-two-pound range, you simply enter 2 lbs. 0 oz under *Item weight and size*. By entering in two pounds, it will cover the postage for items that weigh in the one-to-two-pound range when shipped.

Remember that packages, not letters, ship within pound ranges. Under one pound, one to two pounds, two to three pounds, etc. The trick is to just enter the highest of the two ranges. For packages that weigh between one and two pounds, you enter in two pounds. For packages that weigh between two and three pounds, you enter in three pounds.

See how easy it is when you only need to know the weight RANGE? Under one pound, one to two pounds, two to three pounds, three to four pounds, etc. When an item is being shipped via *Ground Advantage, Priority Mail,* or *Media Mail,* you only need to know the RANGE of weight. There is no need to worry about being exact down to the ounce. Just round it up to the largest pound, and you are good to go!

Remember that you also need to factor packing materials into the weight of your item. Yes, packing paper, newspaper, bubble wrap, packing peanuts, enclosures, and tape will add additional weight to the shipment. For example, let's say you are selling an antique depression glass vase. In a shipping box, the vase weighs 2 pound 11 ounces. However, you will need to use quite a bit of packing materials to ensure the vase doesn't break during shipment. The packing materials will likely push the weight of the package over 2 pounds, meaning you would have to enter 3 pounds as the shipping weight.

PRO TIP: The chances of the Post Office weighing your packages is slim, but it does happen. Sometimes packages are pulled at random to be weighed or a box might need to be sent through the scanner twice, triggering a new weigh-in. In all of the years I've been selling online, I've only had one package be returned to me for insufficient postage, and it was very early on in my business. And I've never had a customer contact me saying they had to pay extra postage for their package to be delivered. Always rounding up has saved both myself and my customers the hassle of dealing with incorrect postage.

Item Size (when packed): The final field to fill out for Etsy shipping is *Item size*. This is an optional field and one you do not have to worry about unless your package is oversized. Packages that measure OVER 36 inches in length and girth combined are oversized. Basically, this means that boxes measuring OVER 12 x 12 x12 inches are oversized. Any size box under that is standard size. And you don't need to enter in standard sizes. I have my default size set to 6x6x6 just because the Etsy system likes to have this field filled out, but it doesn't actually mean anything when it comes to printing labels.

Printing Labels: An order has come in! It's time to print the shipping label and send the package to the customer.

To find new orders, go to your *Etsy Shop Manager* by clicking on the small "store" icon at the top of the page. On the left side of the page, you'll see a bar of options. Look for the orange circle with a number in it next to **Orders & Shipping** - this indicates that you have orders to ship. Click on *Orders & Shipping* to view them.

Note that you can print shipping labels in bulk by selecting all the orders. However, let's go through the process of shipping one order at a time. The first time you ship anything can be stressful since it's a new process, but it will become second nature once you've shipped out a few orders. And to be honest, when it comes to shipping multiple orders of varying sizes, I still do each one by one!

All your orders will be in one section on this page, with each order shown inside a box with a line around it. Hover your mouse over the box to shade it and click anywhere in the shaded area to open a pop-up window.

Click on the black **Get shipping labels** button, which will open up a new window with shipping details, such as weight and postage method, that you entered when creating the listing. Those choices have already been pre-selected. However, if you need to change anything, such as the package type, weight, box size, or delivery service, you can do so here before you purchase the label.

PRO TIP: Even though you didn't need to enter a package size when creating your listing, sometimes Etsy will require it when printing the actual label. If the package is shipping within the United States via *Priority Mail, Media Mail,* or *Parcel Select,* the size of the box only matters if it is over 36 inches combined. Boxes measuring 12x12x12 inches or less do not need exact measurements, so, for domestic shipments, you can put any measurements you want. However, if you can enter the exact measurements, there is no reason not to. Most boxes come printed with their measurements on the bottom. If you're shipping internationally, exact measurements may be necessary to calculate the correct shipping cost. This is why you always want to keep a tape measurer close to your postage scale!

Once everything on the screen is correct, click **Review.** A new screen will pop up showing you the cost of the label you're about to purchase.

This cost will be added to your Etsy bill, and Etsy will automatically deduct it from your balance.

Click on the **Purchase** icon. A new pop-up screen will appear. Click on **Print shipping labels** and then click on the **Print** icon on the screen. Another pop-up screen with the label will appear. Choose the printer you want to print the label from, and then click **Print.**

Once the label has been printed, close the screen. You'll now be back on the screen where you choose *Print shipping labels*. You'll also see an option to **Print packing slips.** I like to print packing slips because they help me stay organized when I'm printing several orders at once, and I think including them in orders gives a professional touch to my business. But the choice to do so is completely up to you.

After printing the label and packing slip, you can go ahead and package your order! Etsy will notify your customer that their order has been processed and give them the tracking number that coordinates to the label you just printed. Once your carrier has scanned in the package, both you and your customer will be able to track it online.

PRO TIP: If you need to reprint or redo any shipping label for any reason, you can do so by going back to the *Orders & Shipping* section and clicking on the *Completed Orders* tab. Here, you'll see all the orders for which you've printed labels. If you need to refund a label and reprint it, whether because the label didn't print correctly or you misplaced it, simply click on the *Refund* link under the tracking number. Etsy will ask you why you want to refund the label. You can then pay for and print a new label. It will take a few days, but you'll eventually be refunded the cost of the first label. Your customer will automatically receive a notification with the new tracking link, and the new tracking information will be updated in your account, too.

Packing orders: Once you have printed the shipping label, you need to package the order. The amount of packing materials you will need depends on what you are selling. If you sell textiles such as vintage clothing and tea towels, you can easily ship those in poly mailing bags with no extra packaging. You simply close up the bag and attach the shipping labels. Jewelry should be put into a protective bag or box but can then be placed inside a small bubble mail envelope without extra padding. Ephemera such as cards and stickers should be placed in a cardboard mailer to prevent them from being bent during shipping.

However, for larger, breakable items, it isn't enough to put the item into a box by itself. You need to protect the item when it is transported during the shipping process.

Box-In-A-Box: Experienced online sellers often talk about the *box-in-a-box* method for shipping. This technique involves creating a boxlike barrier between your product and the shipping box to protect it during transit. If you're a frequent online shopper, you've probably received boxes in various states of disarray. The *box-in-a-box* method helps prevent damage to your product caused by damage to the shipping box itself. This method is especially important if you're shipping breakable items such as pottery and ceramics, or materials that can easily dent such a tin or metal.

To use the *box-in-a-box* method for breakable items, start by wrapping your item in bubble wrap. I recommend that you use at least two layers of bubble wrap for added protection, more if the item is glass or porcelain. Then, use cardboard rolls, which you can purchase on Amazon, to wrap around the bubble wrap. This creates a box-like barrier around your item. Use plenty of packing materials, such as packing peanuts, shredded paper, and/or packing paper, to secure the item in the shipping box.

PRO TIP: If your item is any type of open container such as a vase, stuff the middle with packing paper. This will help protect the piece from shattering internally.

My test to see if an item is packaged well is to shake the shipping box. If nothing rattles around, it's packaged well. If I can feel the item shifting, I open up the box and put more packing material inside. Delivery people often throw boxes into their trucks and onto porches, so, in my opinion, you can't really overpack an order. However, remember that the more packing materials you use, the more the box will weigh.

Here are some additional tips for packing Etsy orders, specifically antiques and vintage collectibles:

Choose the right box: Make sure you choose a box that is sturdy enough to protect your items during shipping. If you're shipping delicate or fragile items, use the box-in-a-box method and also add in extra padding. While it's fine to repurpose clean boxes, be sure the boxes are good for shipping breakables. For example, Amazon shipping boxes tend to be very lightweight. While they can be repurposed for some items, they aren't always the best choice for shipping glass or pottery.

Wrap, wrap, wrap: Wrap your items in bubble wrap or packing paper to prevent them from moving around in the box during shipping. You can also use tissue paper or shredded paper for extra cushioning on items that aren't in danger of breaking. Cardboard rolls also provide an added layer of protection. I keep packing peanuts on hand for extra fragile items. I save every bit of clean packing material I get in my own online shopping orders to reuse for shipping the items I sell.

Add a personal touch...or not: Etsy promotes sellers adding a handwritten note or a pre-printed thank you card along with a small freebie to thank your customer for their purchase. I am not an advocate of handwritten notes as it is a time-consuming step. However, you can have thank you cards printed up with a general "Thank you for your order!" and your Etsy shop URL. I used to order business cards from Vistaprint for this purpose.

These days, I like to include the packing slip that I printed from Etsy along with a free sticker or magnet that features my shop URL. I find that stickers and magnets are a better choice than regular cards as buyers are more likely to use them rather than throw them away. I order my stickers and magnets from Sticker Mule. I create my designs in Canva and then upload them to Sticker Mule for printing.

Use clear tape: Use clear shipping tape (remember, the best deals are at Sam's Club and Costco, although you can also find good prices on Amazon) to seal the box securely. Make sure to tape all the seams and edges to prevent the box from coming apart during shipping. If you are using a label you printed out on paper, it is okay to put some clear tape over the edges of the shipping label, but don't put tape over the bar code as it can interfere with the Post Office being able to scan your package into their system.

Do not wrap the shipping box: New sellers sometimes make the mistake of wrapping their boxes in brown paper. Not only is this a waste of time and money, but it is also against postal guidelines as the edges of the paper can get stuck in the sorting machines. If you are repurposing a box and want to cover up printing that is on it, consider using brown packing tape or stickers. If the package is being shipped via Priority Mail, you can use the free Priority Mail stickers from the Post Office to cover things up.

Mailing orders: Once you've secured the shipping label to your package, it's time to get it into the hands of the USPS. There are two ways to do this: drive your packages to your local Post Office or schedule a free Carrier Pickup.

If you choose to take your packages to the Post Office, you have a couple of options. You can go inside the building and wait in line to have a postal clerk scan your packages in. Or you can drive around the back of the building to the loading dock to unload your packages without having to wait in line. My Post Office has a dedicated dock where people can leave packages. However, every Post Office location has its own policies, so make sure to ask before leaving your packages.

If you only have a few packages, you may be able to leave them inside at the counter without having to wait in line. Again, ask what's easiest for the employees and be accommodating. Remember, these people are an essential part of your business, and being kind and polite can go a long way. My Post Office clerks encourage me to leave my packages for them to scan later, but some locations do not allow this.

Your second option is to schedule a free pickup at your home or place of business from your postal carrier. Scheduling a free Carrier Pickup from the USPS is a great option for online sellers who have a large number of packages or who are unable to make it to the Post Office during business hours. It's especially helpful if you have packages every day that need to be shipped. To schedule a pickup, visit tool.usps.com/schedule-pickup-steps.

You can schedule package pickups Monday through Saturday, the same days that Mail Carriers deliver the mail. If you have a small number of packages, your regular carrier will likely collect them. However, if you have a large number of outgoing orders, the Post Office may send a mail truck out to pick them up. You must be prepared for your packages to be picked up at any time. I have a deck box on my porch where I put my outgoing packages. This protects them from the elements as well as from being stolen. I leave a note on my mailbox directing whoever is picking up the packages as to where they are.

PRO TIP: If you have a lot of outgoing Etsy orders for your USPS carrier to collect, and if you are getting numerous packages of supplies to run your shop, consider leaving snacks out for your delivery drivers. I have a box filled with pre-packed candy bars, chips, and cookies that I leave out for those who collect and deliver packages to my home. I buy these snacks in bulk from Sam's Club. All of the delivery people who come to my house appreciate these. However, I have to hide them from the street view as I've had them stolen off my porch from kids walking home from school.

Tracking: Etsy will notify your customer when their package has shipped. There is no need to message your customer directly unless there is an issue with their order. If you printed the shipping label on Etsy, the tracking for the package will automatically upload for both you and your customer.

And that's it! You have shipped your first Etsy order! Trust me that after you have shipped out a few packages, the process will become easier. Once the package has been scanned in at your buyer's location, Etsy will release the funds from the sale to your account. And when you start to see your Etsy balance build, you'll wonder why you waited so long to sell online!

CHAPTER EIGHT: MARKETING YOUR ETSY SHOP

If you have been selling your antiques locally, you may already have some advertising in place. Perhaps you have a booth at an antique mall or sell on the flea market circuit and have a name for your business along with business cards and signage. However, to grow your business on Etsy, you will need to shift your focus from marketing locally to advertising online. Fortunately, marketing antiques online is easy thanks to social media platforms. And in many cases, these options are also free.

In this chapter, we'll discuss the various social media sites and how you can utilize each to drive traffic to your Etsy shop. We'll also talk about some paid options you can consider. But first, just another reminder that the best thing you can do to advertise your business is to maximize Etsy SEO.

Are you tired of me harping on Etsy SEO? If you are, I don't blame you. But it is the best thing you can do to drive traffic to your Etsy shop and make sales. Remember that SEO (*Search Engine Optimization*) involves repeating relevant keywords in your titles, descriptions, tags, and shop sections. This repetition of keywords tells Etsy that they need to focus on those keywords when putting your items into their search algorithm.

When done effectively, SEO can help your Etsy products to rank higher in search results and increase the chances of them being seen by potential customers. And effective use of SEO can eliminate the need to run expensive *Etsy Ads*. Once I mastered Etsy SEO, I stopped using *Etsy Ads*, which are the ads you pay for whenever someone clicks on them. I do, however, opt into *Etsy Off-Site Ads* as I only pay for those ads when a click leads to a sale.

It can't be said enough that maximizing Etsy SEO is the number one tool you must utilize to bring customers to your shop. Researching the best keywords for your products and using those keywords in your titles, descriptions, tags, shop sections, and even in areas where you can customize your shop's announcements and information will tell Etsy that they need to be pushing your products to customers searching those keywords.

Is it annoying that you can't just write a good title and be done with the listing? Yes. Is it tempting to just focus on a keyword-loaded title and call it a day the same way Amazon, eBay, and Poshmark sellers do with their listings? Yes. But unfortunately, this isn't the reality of selling on Etsy. Repeating the most important keywords that pertain to your listings is the best thing you can do to bring shoppers to your listings and turn those shoppers into paying customers.

However, although SEO plays a significant role in helping customers discover your products on platforms such as Google and on the Etsy site itself, there are additional strategies you can utilize to drive traffic to your listings. The good news is that most of these tactics are not only fast and easy but also free. This is because these methods involve leveraging social media platforms to grow your business.

Back in the early days of e-commerce, there were only a handful of shopping websites available, and customers had limited options for purchasing items online. When I started selling online, eBay and Amazon were the only online shopping websites available. I was able to easily sell on both platforms for several years as there was little competition. Since customers had only two choices when it came to online shopping, I didn't have to compete for their attention. Shoppers came to me because I was one of the few online sellers. I didn't even need to have the best product pictures, titles, or descriptions. I could just take a couple of photos and list products for sale without doing any advertising.

However, the e-commerce landscape has changed significantly since I began selling online in 2005. There are now thousands of online shopping websites available. Every single brand and retail store has an e-commerce website. And numerous "reselling" platforms have emerged alongside eBay and Amazon, including Etsy, Poshmark, Mercari, Facebook Marketplace, TikTok Shops, and WhatNot. Not to mention small brands and individual sellers who create their own websites through platforms such as Shopify and Wix to sell directly to customers. This increase in online competition means that simply listing products for sale is no longer enough to make sales. You have to put in extra work to bring shoppers to your listings.

Etsy is an especially competitive marketplace. It is no longer just for crafters. Vintage and antique sellers, sticker shops, print-on-demand drop shipping, and digital downloads are all a huge part of Etsy's offerings. Your antiques will appear alongside competitor listings from sellers not only offering the exact same items as you are, but also from shops that sell tee shirts, clip art, and eBooks that are similar in theme to the antiques you have listed. This means that you as a seller are not only competing against other antique dealers but all of the other shops on Etsy, too.

For instance, if you specialize in vintage Christmas items, you will be competing with other shops that sell Christmas antiques. But you will also be competing with shops that sell anything for Christmas, including handmade items such as crafts or digital downloads. A shopper may have come on to Etsy to search for vintage Christmas collectibles but strayed into the shop of someone who sells custom Christmas cards. Or they may have seen your listing for a vintage

Christmas figurine but saw another seller with the same figurine but whose listing was priced lower.

Because so many people are now selling on Etsy, it is important to think of your Etsy shop as a brand, and not just a platform you use to sell on. The category and niches you focus on, the antiques you sell, and the aesthetic of your photos should all have a cohesive look and theme that contributes to your brand identity. While some antique dealers sell a little bit of everything, many of us specialize in a handful of categories. Sellers who specialize in Mid Century Modern items tend to have a colorful art deco look to their shop, while sellers of primitives focus on earthy tones.

PRO TIP: If you are an antique dealer who specializes in several distinct niches, you may want to consider opening separate Etsy shops for each. An example would be a seller who sells a lot of vintage jewelry but also sells a lot of retro toys. Creating two different Etsy shops, one for each of these categories, may be more effective in bringing in customers than putting all items into one shop. While the one-stop shop method works great on eBay, it can hold you back on Etsy. Etsy shoppers look at online shops just as they would a brick-and-mortar store. A cohesive look and a focused product line can help you stand out over other sellers whose stores are a hodgepodge of all sorts of things.

Now, that's not to say that an Etsy shop can't have a mix of items. Many sellers sell a wide variety of items in their shops. However, if you have two or three distinct niches you focus on, a second or even third Etsy shop may work best. I would recommend starting with one shop and, if you feel it necessary, branch out to another one down the road. You can have as many Etsy shops as you'd like, but you do need to create separate accounts with different email addresses for each.

Once you have mastered Etsy SEO and have done all you can to bring in shoppers who are already on Etsy, you can turn your attention to bringing in customers from other websites. And the first place you will want to start is on Facebook.

Facebook: To establish your brand, you must create a Facebook business page. Facebook has a user base of nearly 3 billion people around the world, making it the ideal platform for reaching new customers. Not only is Facebook free to use, but it's also user-friendly. While other social media sites, like TikTok, are gaining momentum, Facebook remains the top choice for businesses as you can reach an older audience of users who have more disposable income to spend on things such as antiques.

To use Facebook to drive traffic to your Etsy store, you'll need to create a **Facebook Business Page**, which is different from a personal Facebook page. With a personal Facebook page, you send and accept friend requests from family and acquaintances. You have the option of keeping your profile entirely private, and you don't need to censor yourself because only those you approve of as "friends" can see your posts.

However, a *Facebook Business Page* is separate from a personal account. Rather than people "friending" you, they will instead need to "like" your page to "follow" you. You need this distinction to separate your personal life from your business, not only to build your brand but to protect your privacy. While you may enjoy discussing politics and religion on your personal Facebook page, you want to refrain from these sometimes-controversial topics when it comes to your business. A business page also protects the privacy of your friends and family as customers won't see their information.

To create a *Facebook Business Page,* you first need to have a personal Facebook account. From there you simply:

1. Go to **facebook.com/about/pages**
2. Log in to your personal Facebook account (even if you were already logged in, Facebook's system will usually have you reenter your login information to confirm your identity)
3. Follow the prompts to create a new business page

The first decision you will need to make is to name your page. I currently have several Facebook pages, including one that serves as my main page as well as pages for my Etsy shop and eBay store. You can create as many business pages as you'd like. Because your business pages are all tied to your personal page, you can easily flip back and forth between them all simply by clicking on the icon in the top right-corner of your Facebook account.

As you create additional social media accounts related to your antique business, it's important to make sure that they all have the same name to establish a cohesive online presence. You will want all your social media account names to match or closely match your Etsy shop name.

For example, I sell journals, planners, notebooks, and adult coloring books on Amazon through their self-publishing platform, Amazon KDP. My pen name for those products is *Jean Lee Publishing*. I decided to name my Etsy sticker and magnet shop *Jean Lee Publishing*, too, so that I could create different products under one "brand name," which has enabled me to have a dedicated website, JeanLeePublishing.com, where customers can choose to visit my Etsy shop or Amazon storefront. Because journal, notebooks, stickers, and magnets all fall under the "stationery" category, having these products under one brand name makes sense.

However, for my antiques and vintage collectibles, which over the years I have sold on eBay, Etsy, and WhatNot, my business name is *Annabella's Gift Shop*. This was the name I had when I first started selling online in 2005, and I have a Facebook page just for that business name.

And I also have a Facebook page for *Ann Eckhart,* which is my actual name and the name I write non-fiction books under. My YouTube channel is also under my name, so I promote my videos on this Facebook page, too.

NOTE: Most people do not have as many Facebook business pages as I do! It is only because I have developed several different businesses over the years that I have so many. It is perfectly normal for you to only have ONE page that is dedicated to your antique business. Many YouTube creators who have channels dedicated to reselling use the same name for their business and channel as well as across all of their social media platforms.

After you have created a Facebook business account, Facebook will prompt you to personalize your page by:

1. **Adding a profile picture:** This is the image that will appear next to your page name and posts. You want to use the same profile picture for your Facebook page that you use for your Etsy shop. Most Etsy sellers choose their shop's logo as their profile picture.
2. **Adding a banner:** This is the large image that appears at the top of your Facebook page. You can create a custom banner on a site like Canva, which has templates already made for Facebook banners. If this type of graphics work isn't something you are comfortable doing, you can hire a designer on a site such as Fiverr.com who can create banners and any other graphics you need.
3. **Customizing your page's tabs:** Facebook allows you to add various tabs to your page, including linking your Etsy shop right on your page.

The **About** section of your Facebook page offers several different fields that you can fill out. Facebook prompts will walk you through this section. However, note that you don't have to complete any of these sections right away or at all if you don't want to. If the main goal is to drive traffic to your Etsy shop, then your Etsy link is the most important link you want on your page.

Once you have set up your Facebook business page, you need to start building your audience by getting people to "like" your page. Facebook will prompt you to invite friends and family from your personal account to "like" your new page and most of the people you are connected with will give your page a follow. However, remember that you can't expect your friends and family to buy from you. To build a business, you need to reach beyond your immediate circle.

While creating a Facebook business page is free, there are some paid options that Facebook offers to help grow your business. Facebook Ads allow you to target specific groups of people who may be interested in your products and encourage them to "like" your page to click through to your Etsy shop.

To create a Facebook ad:

1. Go to your Facebook business page and click on the **Create** button at the top of the page.
2. From the drop-down menu, select **Ad** to create a new ad campaign.
3. **Choose your ad objective.** Facebook offers a range of ad objectives to choose from, including "Website Visits," "Conversions," "Product Catalog Sales," and more. I recommend "Website Visits" because, after all, the goal is to bring customers to your Etsy shop.
4. **Set up your targeting options.** Facebook allows you to target specific groups of people based on demographics,

interests, behaviors, and more. Use the targeting options to narrow down your audience to the people most likely to be interested in your products. You can do this by typing in keywords that relate to your products.

5. **Select your ad placements.** You can choose to show your ad on Facebook, Instagram, or both, as well as on other platforms such as "Audience Network" and "Marketplace." I choose all options so that my ad has the widest reach.

6. **Set your budget and schedule.** Decide how much you want to spend on your ad campaign and over what period. You can choose to run your ad continuously or set specific start and end dates. I usually start with $5 a day to test the ad.

7. **Create your ad.** Use the ad creation tools to design your ad, including the ad format, images, text, and call-to-action (CTA) button. You can choose from a variety of ad formats, including single images, carousels, and videos. I recommend adding a few of your best-selling product photos.

8. **Review and submit your ad.** Once you have finished creating your ad, review all the details to make sure everything is correct. When you are ready, click **Submit** to create your ad campaign.

The **Boost Post** feature on Facebook is another paid advertising tool that allows you to promote a specific post from your Facebook business page to a larger audience. This is an easier method than creating an ad from scratch. For example, I often share direct links to new listings on my Facebook pages. I can then simply "boost" specific posts rather than create an ad from scratch.

To **boost a post from your Facebook business page**, follow these steps:

1. Go to your Facebook business page and find the post that

you want to promote.

2. Click on the **Boost Post** button below the post.

3. **Select your target audience.** You can choose to show your boosted post to people who already like your page, to a specific group of people based on demographics and interests, or to a custom audience that you define. I usually choose to have the post shown to people who "like" my page and their friends and family. This way the people they are connected to will see that their friend or family member "likes" my business, which can encourage them to check it out.

4. **Set your budget and duration**. Decide how much you want to spend on your boosted post and over what period. You can choose to boost your post for as little as $1 per day or as much as you want. I like to choose a seven-day option with a budget of no more than $35 ($5 per day) to test how the ad performs.

5. **Review and boost your post.** Once you have finished setting up your boosted post, review all the details to make sure everything is correct. When you are ready, click **Boost** to promote your post.

Do you need to pay for advertising on Facebook? When it comes to selling antiques, my opinion is usually no. Because you will usually only have one of each item you are selling, it's hard to create an ad or even boost a post as what you advertise may sell out while the ad is still running. If you want to get more followers to your page, then running an ad may work. But overall, you should only consider an ad if you have something really special to advertise, such as if you are running a big sale or if you have just listed a large collection of similar items. For example, if you acquire and list dozens of pieces of Fenton, a Facebook ad may help drive customers to your shop. But for most resellers, simply sharing their new Etsy listings to their Facebook pages is enough advertising.

Creating Content: So, you have set up a Facebook page for your business and have started getting people to "like" it. Now you need to commit to posting regular content on your page to keep your followers engaged. Creating engagement isn't just about seeing followers see your posts but also interacting with them by clicking the "thumbs up" button, leaving comments, or sharing your posts on their Facebook feeds to get their friends and family to like your page, too.

I always share my newest listings directly to my Facebook page, which Etsy makes easy to do. To **share an Etsy listing on your Facebook page**, follow these steps:

1. Go to your Etsy shop and find the listing that you want to share.
2. Click on the **Share** button below the listing.
3. Select **Facebook** from the drop-down menu.
4. A pop-up window will appear, asking you to log in to your Facebook account. Enter your login credentials and click **Log In.**
5. A new window will appear, allowing you to customize the message that will be posted to your Facebook page along with the listing. You can add a message or simply leave the default message.
6. When you are ready, click **Post to Facebook** to share the listing on your Facebook page.

In addition to promoting your Etsy listings on Facebook, find other ways to engage with your followers. You can do this by posting updates about new inventory, running polls, doing giveaways, or sharing relevant information such as deadlines for holiday orders. Even posting holiday messages and reminders about events is an easy way to keep your page active.

Remember that when people engage with your Facebook posts, Facebook may show the engagement in that person's feed so that their friends can see it. And those friends, seeing that they know someone who follows your page, may decide to follow your page, too. Therefore, it is important to keep your posts positive and avoid posting about controversial or offensive topics. In other words, unless you are selling religious or political-themed products, avoid those two topics. The goal of your business page is to attract customers and make money. Posting about sensitive subjects can turn people away.

However, that's not to say you can't have non-business content on your Facebook business page. Sharing a picture of you shopping at a flea market or showing your personal collections of vintage treasures can often bring more engagement than posting a new listing. A picture of your pet, a funny quote, wishing your customers a "happy-whatever-holiday-it-is", or even a photo of your lunch can go a long way toward building rapport with your followers. And the more rapport you have with your followers, the more likely they are to turn into customers.

Twitter: Like Facebook, Twitter is another free social media platform that you can use to promote your Etsy shop. With Twitter, you can share short updates, called "tweets," with your followers and engage with them through **@replies** and **#hashtags.**

If you don't already have a Twitter account, you can create one for free at Twitter.com. Note that if you have an existing personal Twitter account that you are active on, you may want to consider creating a separate account for your Etsy business to keep your personal and professional lives separate. You can create multiple Twitter accounts; you just need to use separate email addresses. And you can easily get new email addresses for free through Google at mail.google.com.

Remember as you are creating social media pages for your Etsy shop to use the same handle for your Twitter account as you have for your Etsy shop and Facebook page to create a consistent online presence for your business. This will make it easier for people to find and follow you across different platforms and helps in building your brand. If your business name is too long or has already been taken, try condensing it or creating a variation. I use both "Jean Lee" and "Jean Lee Publishing" for Etsy and Amazon, as well as on the social media pages for that business.

Twitter limits their "tweets" to 280 characters or less. This is an increase from the original 140 characters, and you want to use every available space offered. Etsy makes it easy to share your listings on Twitter by including a share button in all active listings. To use the Twitter share button, simply click on it within a listing, and a new window will open on Twitter with the title of your listing and the direct link to it already populated. You can send the "tweet" as is or customize the message as well as add hashtags.

Hashtags (marked as such with the # sign) are a way to categorize and organize content on social media platforms, especially on Twitter and Instagram. In fact, I find that hashtags are more useful on Twitter than on any other platform as users are more accustomed to using them there than on other sites. Twitter users can follow their favorite hashtags to keep up with the posts they are most interested in seeing.

Hashtags that are popular for Etsy antique shops include:

- #etsy
- #etsy
- #etsyshop
- #etsyseller
- #antiques
- #vintage

- #VintageStyle
- #EtsyAntiques
- #AntiqueShop
- #AntiqueLovers
- #VintageDecor
- #VintageEtsy
- #midcenturymodern
- #retro

Adding hashtags to your "tweets" is an easy way to increase the chance of your posts being found by interested shoppers. By adding relevant hashtags to your tweets, you are making it easier for people to discover your Etsy business and perhaps buy your items.

For example, let's say you are selling a vintage Lenox Christmas ornament on Etsy. When you click on the Twitter icon in your Etsy listing, your title and the link to the listing will automatically populate to Twitter. If there is room to add more text, you can add hashtags such as #etsy, #etsyshop, #christmas, #lenox, and #vintage.

It's important not to overuse hashtags or use ones that are not relevant to your business. This can make your tweets seem spammy and could turn people off. Instead, choose around five relevant hashtags that accurately describe your business and the products you are selling. While the bridal category is huge on Etsy, don't use the hashtag #bridal in your listings unless the item you are selling is a vintage wedding collectible.

As with sharing your Facebook page with customers, you also want to share your Twitter handle, both online and offline, to encourage them to follow you on the platform. Including your Twitter handle in your other social media profiles and on any other promotional materials will help your customers find you. The @ symbol allows you to easily share your Twitter handle as typing it into Twitter's search bar will take users to your profile.

One way to build up your followers on Twitter is to follow other Twitter users and engage with their content. Some users follow everyone who follows them, which can help increase your follower count. You can also use Twitter's @reply and retweet features to engage with other users and share their content with your followers. This can help build relationships and expose your content to a wider audience. Be sure to network with other resellers on Twitter by following their accounts. And search for users who are avid collectors as you may be able to turn those people into customers.

Instagram: Like Facebook, Instagram is a free-to-use social media platform that allows users to share photos and videos and engage with their followers. Just as with a Facebook business page, Instagram users "follow" accounts they like to see that person's posts in their feed. In fact, Facebook's parent company META owns both Facebook and Instagram, so there is some built-in overlap between the two sites, specifically when it comes to advertising. You can even enable your Instagram posts to be automatically shared on your Facebook page, which eliminates the extra step of manually posting to Facebook.

PRO TIP: Because Facebook owns Instagram, you can connect your accounts so that your Instagram posts will automatically share to your Facebook business page. This is a great time saver as you don't have to create two different posts for each site. Post once on Instagram and the post will share on Facebook automatically. This works for static posts, stories, and reels.

There are several features on Instagram that you can use to share your content about your Etsy shop:

Instagram Posts: *Instagram Posts* are static photos that you share on your profile. They are visible to all your followers and remain on your profile indefinitely unless you delete them. *Instagram Posts* are an easy way to share the images of your products, which is easy to do by simply reposting the same images to Instagram that you use in your Etsy listings. Etsy doesn't have a feature that allows you to share listings to your static posts, so you will need to save a photo to your camera roll to post it on Instagram. I keep a stockpile of photos on my phone so that I always have something to post.

Instagram Stories: *Instagram Stories* are photos or videos that you share on your profile that disappear after 24 hours. *Instagram Stories* are a good way to share behind-the-scenes glimpses of your business, sneak peeks of new products, or more personal content that you may want to share with your followers but that doesn't need to remain on your profile indefinitely.

For example, while I want pictures of my products to always appear on my profile page, I don't need to permanently save a short video of me packing an order or shopping at an estate sale. Note that you can also share your static posts to your *Stories* to make sure those posts get maximum exposure. This makes it easy to get two posts out of one as one static post can also be shared to your *Stories*.

Instagram Reels: *Instagram Reels* allows users to create and share short video clips of up to one minute and thirty seconds that can be edited with music, effects, and custom text. *Instagram Reels* are a great way to create and share fun content that highlights your products. As with static posts, you can also share *Instagram Reels* to your *Instagram Stories*.

PRO TIP: If you have multiple Instagram accounts (you can have as many accounts as you'd like as long as you use a different email address to sign up for each), make sure you cross-post your content across all of your accounts. I have two Instagram pages: one under my name and one for my *Jean Lee Publishing* brand. When I post something on the *Jean Lee Publishing* page, I switch to my other account and share that post to my *Stories*. Since different people follow me on each of my pages, this is a quick and easy way for me to reach more potential customers than if I only posted on one account.

In addition to using Instagram to promote your Etsy listings, you can also use the platform to connect with other resellers as well as your customers on a more personal level by sharing photos that may not always relate directly to your business. For example, you can post photos of your office, video clips from sourcing trips, and other behind-the-scenes glimpses of your shop. Selling antiques gives you a lot of potential content to share, much more so than sellers of other products such as clothing or digital products as you have access to one-of-a-kind treasures that are more likely to create engagement with your followers. After all, who doesn't get excited to see pictures of gorgeous vintage Christmas ornaments or colorful antique depression glass?

Instagram is very much a visual platform, so sharing photos of your pets, meals, or other fun snapshots from your daily life can give your followers a more personal look at who you are, which helps them form a connection to you and makes them more likely to shop your store. Remember, however, that you are using Instagram to promote your Etsy shop. Just as with your other social media business pages, you should avoid sharing controversial or offensive content. And be careful about giving out too much personal information. I carefully guard photos of the front of my house, for instance, for security reasons.

Just as you use hashtags on Twitter, they are also a useful tool on Instagram. Make sure to use hashtags that are relevant to your business and the content you are sharing. This will help ensure that your posts are seen by users who are interested in what you are selling. As an Etsy antique shop, stick to hashtags related to the vintage collectibles you are selling. Many people will use hashtags that have nothing to do with their Etsy shop to be seen by more users. But this can backfire if those users are annoyed seeing your content in their feed and react negatively by leaving angry comments under your posts.

Using popular hashtags can help increase the visibility of your content, but using too many popular hashtags can make it harder for your content to stand out. Consider using a mix of hashtags to balance visibility and relevance. For example, you want to use the hashtags #etsy and #etsyshop in most of your Instagram posts. But also add hashtags of the theme of the products you are posting about. If you are listing mid-century modern décor, you will want to add the hashtags #midcenturymodern and #mcm to your posts, along with the type of item you are selling, such as #glass or #ceramics.

Narrowing down the hashtags you want to include can be a challenge as there are so many potential options. For instance, if you are selling vintage jewelry, possible hashtags could include:

- #etsy
- #etsyshop
- #jewelry
- #vintage
- #vintagejewelry
- #vintagenecklace
- #vintageearrings
- #vintagering
- #vintagebrooch
- #necklace
- #earrings
- #ring

- #brooch

And don't forget hashtags that include the jewelry maker, the metal and materials, and the era. With limited character space on most platforms, you can't include every possible hashtag, meaning you will need to narrow down your choices.

Utilizing a site such as EtsyCheck or eRank can help you find the best hashtags to use. I like to use a mix of popular and more niche hashtags to reach the widest audience possible. I use both EtsyCheck and eRank to find keywords for my listings and hashtags for my social media, along with researching what products are trending on Etsy. I keep a list of hashtags in the *Notes* section of my iPhone to easily copy and paste relevant hashtags to my Instagram posts.

For example, if I am promoting my Etsy sticker shop, I will always use the hashtags #etsy, #etsyshop, and #etsystickershop. But I will then use hashtags related to the sticker I am posting about. If I'm sharing a sticker of a vintage telephone, I may use the hashtags #vintagestickers, #vintagetelephone, or #antiquephone. I always include Etsy-specific hashtags but then find a few that match the product I am selling.

The reason you utilize hashtags is because collectors, the people who will pay top dollar for items, follow specific hashtags. If you are selling a Blenko vase, you want to include the hashtags #blenko, #blenkoglass, #vintageglass, and #blenkocollector. Use all of the available characters to add as many hashtags as possible to cast a wide net for users to find your listings.

Another way to grow your Instagram following is to connect with other Etsy sellers. You can find fellow Etsy shops using the hashtags #etsyshop and #etsyseller. The reselling community is very welcoming on Instagram, and it's not hard to make connections with other antique sellers. Sellers of vintage collectibles love to learn from one another and to see what each other is selling. And antique sellers are also buyers. You may find yourself selling to other dealers who are trying to fill in their collections. Search for the hashtags #reselling, #reseller, and #resellercommunity to find others who sell secondhand and vintage goods online.

Linking your shop: While you can add one live clickable website link to your Instagram profile, you cannot add a live link to your Etsy shop in static Instagram posts, meaning if you add your Etsy shop's URL, it won't be clickable for users. Therefore, to drive traffic to your Etsy listings on Instagram in static posts, you need to include a message in the caption that directs your followers to your profile page, where they can find an active link to your Etsy shop. For example, you can write *Several new retro kitschy collectibles have been added to my Etsy shop! Link to my store is in my bio at @yourinstagramhandle!*

By including the @ symbol and your Instagram handle, you will create a clickable link that will take users to your profile page, where they can click on the link to your Etsy shop and browse your listings. And while you can't add live links to static posts, you can add a live clickable link in your Instagram stories by using the **Link** option.

If you want to share multiple links on Instagram, not just the link to your Etsy shop, you will need to use a service like **Linktr.ee** to create a landing page that allows you to list all your links in one place. With a *Linktr.ee* page, you can add as many links as you like, allowing users to be able to access them all by clicking on the main *Linktr.ee* link in your Instagram profile. To see an example, visit my *Linktr.ee* page at **linktr.ee/anneckhart.**

To grow your Instagram following, aim to post something every single day. An easy way to start this habit is to post a picture of one new item in your Etsy shop as a static post. Then "share" that static post to your *Instagram Stories* and add the direct link to the listing. And also take time to engage with other accounts by liking and commenting on their posts.

Pinterest: Pinterest is a social media platform for sharing and discovering ideas and inspiration by "pinning" images and videos to virtual boards. Pinterest "boards" allow users to "pin" posts, similar to how one uses a bulletin board. Users create different "boards" for different categories and niches. Antiques and vintage, especially certain collectible niches, are popular on Pinterest, so sharing your Etsy listings there just makes since. And as a bonus, it's not only easy but free!

As with Facebook and Twitter, Etsy includes a share button in all active listings that makes it easy to share your listings on Pinterest. You can share your Etsy listings on specific boards that you have created that relate to your category and various niches. If, like me, you sell a wide variety of items across multiple categories, you could create a board for each. For example, a board for glass, a board for jewelry, a board for figurines, and so one. You can also pin listings to multiple boards. For example, if you are listing a Christmas figurine, you could post it to a board for figurines and a board for Christmas.

As with the other social media platforms, you can use hashtags to make it easier for people to discover your Pinterest boards, although hashtags aren't used as much on Pinterest as they are on other sites. Pinterest is much more of a visual platform, so rather than worry too much about hashtags, you want your focus to be on making sure the pictures you share are the best quality you have.

Finding content on Pinterest that coordinates with your products and re-pinning those posts as well as following their creators is another way to connect with not only other accounts but also the people who follow those accounts. If you sell a lot of Fenton, search for Fenton boards and follow those. If your specialty is vintage Christmas, search out those boards. Doing this allows you to connect with shoppers who follow those boards, which will lead them to your Etsy shop.

If you do create a Pinterest account, be sure to share the link with your customers and followers on other social media platforms and any promotional materials. You can easily add your Pinterest URL to the links section of your Facebook business page as well as to your Linktr.ee if you have one.

TikTok: TikTok is the newest social media platform that allows users to create and share short videos, also referred to as "short-form content." TikTok began with a younger demographic but is slowly growing with users of all ages. On TikTok, users can create short videos (up to three minutes) that can be edited with music, effects, and other creative tools. From comedy skits and dances to personal stories and small business, there are TikTok videos for every interest.

Since TikTok relies on short-form videos, antique sellers have an immediate advantage when it comes to creating content. You can share your latest finds and sales as well as clips of you out shopping at garage sales, estate sales, flea markets, and thrift stores. You can use your TikTok page to simply promote your Etsy shop, but if you are passionate about certain collectibles, you can also use the platform as a teaching tool to share your knowledge.

The best part about using TikTok for your Etsy shop is that it is strictly made for use on mobile devices, meaning you use your smartphone, not a computer, to film and engage on the platform. TikTok offers several tutorials right on their app to walk you through the process. You can film, edit, and upload right on the app, which helps save time over piecing clips together from several sources.

There are a lot of Etsy shop owners on TikTok, so it won't be hard for you to find other sellers to connect with. Search the hashtags #etsyshop and #etsyseller to connect with other shop owners. But also search for #vintage, #antiques, #collector, and hashtags related to the items you sell to find shoppers who may be interested in what you have for sale.

There are two types of TikTok accounts for users to choose from: personal and business. A **TikTok personal account** is an account that is for, you guessed it, personal use. Most personal account users aren't interested in growing a large following on the app and are on TikTok just for fun. Many don't even post videos, they just have an account that enables them to scroll the app while being able to like, comment, and share their favorite clips.

A **TikTok business account**, however, is an account that is specifically designed for businesses, both small and large. Business accounts on TikTok have access to features and tools that are not available for personal account users, such as analytics and advertising. It is free to create either a personal or business TikTok account, so there is no reason not to start out strong with a business account for your Etsy shop.

The biggest benefit of a TikTok business account is that you can put a clickable URL in your profile. Personal account users cannot put a clickable link in their profile; only business account users can. I have my Linktr.ee link in my TikTok business account profile, which will take people to a static page with all of my business links, including a link to my Etsy shop. Remember that your main goal when using social media is to drive traffic to your Etsy shop. And a clickable link makes that much easier to do as users won't have to log out of TikTok, log onto Etsy, and then manually search for your shop.

Note that you can create multiple TikTok pages under one account. If you already have a personal account, you can easily add a second account for your business. It's a simple process to switch back and forth between your multiple accounts without having to constantly log out and back in.

To create a TikTok business account for an Etsy shop, follow these steps:

1. **Download the TikTok app** on your phone or tablet.
2. Open the app and tap on the **Me** icon in the bottom right corner.
3. Tap on the **three dots** in the top right corner and select **Manage account**.
4. Tap on **Switch to Professional Account**.
5. Select **Business** as the account type.
6. Follow the prompts to complete the account setup process, including adding your business name, contact information, and any other required information.

There are several ways you can use TikTok to promote your Etsy business:

Create and share posts about your products: Use TikTok's creative tools and features, such as music, effects, and filters, to create short (no longer than one minute is ideal but you can make videos as short as 15 seconds and as long as 3 minutes) videos that highlight your vintage listings. Sharing new inventory is a great way to drive traffic to your shop, but you don't want every post to be a direct sales pitch. Offering advice about buying and collecting antiques is a great way to gain followers and create engagement. Short video clips of you sourcing new products and shipping out orders are also popular with TikTok users.

Participate in trends: TikTok is famous for trending dances, challenges, and filters. Participating in these is a fun and easy way to create engagement. While the trends may not have anything to do with your business, because they are so popular, your posts are bound to get more views. Make sure to only participate in trends that are non-controversial and won't harm your business image. Finding a way to incorporate your antique business into these trends is also helpful. Follow other resellers on the app to see how they are tying their reselling activities to popular trends.

Use relevant hashtags and tags: Just like with Twitter and Instagram, by including relevant hashtags and tags in your TikTok posts, you can make it easier for users to discover your content and interact with your account as well as hopefully visit your Etsy shop. The hashtags #etsy, #etsyshop, #etsyseller, #antiques, #vintage, #collectibles, #reselling, and #reseller will help you connect with buyers as well as others in the reselling community.

As I mentioned in the Instagram section of this chapter, I keep a list of hashtags in the notes section of my phone that I just copy and paste into posts. TikTok allows you to write up to 2,200 characters in the caption of a post. However, it's worth noting that descriptions on TikTok are rarely read, as the main focus is on the video content and the related hashtags rather than the written text. A caption of around 100-200 characters is considered optimal for TikTok, as it allows for enough text to add context and engage with the audience, but still keeps the focus on the video. However, there are many times I only add hashtags with no other text. If I do add text, I prefer to do so using captions that appear on the actual video.

TikTok's advertising features: TikTok's business accounts have access to advertising features that can help you reach a wider audience beyond those who follow your account and thus drive traffic to your Etsy shop. You can create and manage ads on TikTok to reach users who are interested in your products or related topics based on their activities on the app, which TikTok tracks. TikTok's advertising opportunities include:

- **In-feed ads:** These are native ads that appear in users' feeds, like sponsored posts on other social media platforms. They can be in the form of videos, photos, or carousels and can include a call-to-action button.
- **Brand takeover ads:** These are full-screen ads that appear when a user opens the app. They can be in the form of a video or image and are a great way to grab users' attention.
- **Branded hashtag challenge:** This feature allows businesses to create a hashtag challenge, which encourages users to create and share content using the designated hashtag.
- **Branded effects:** TikTok's AR effects allow businesses to create their own branded filters and lenses that users can use in their videos.
- **Branded hashtag stickers:** These are branded stickers that users can use in their videos and are associated with a specific hashtag.

To access TikTok's advertising platform, you will need to sign up for a **TikTok Ads** account. Here's how you can do that:

1. Go to the TikTok Ads website at **tiktok.com/business/ad-center**.
2. Click on the **Sign-Up** button in the top right corner of the page.
3. Fill in the required information to create a new account, including your name, email address, and password.

Once you have created your account, you can access TikTok's advertising platform by logging in to the TikTok Ads website and clicking on the **Create** button in the top right corner of the page. From there, you can choose the type of ad you want to create and follow the prompts to set up your campaign. As with any advertising, I always recommend starting with a small budget and only increasing it if you see results.

YouTube: Starting a YouTube channel can be a great way to promote your reselling business and thus drive traffic to your Etsy shop. There is an active reselling community on YouTube. Creators film videos of themselves shopping at antique malls and thrift stores, hauls of their finds, and offer tips and tricks for listing and shipping. I film videos of myself shopping at estate sales, and I also show items as they sell. These videos help drive traffic to my online stores and generate sales.

Don't have a fancy camera? No problem as you don't need a digital camera to film YouTube videos. I use my iPhone to film my YouTube videos as well as all of my social media content. I also use my iPhone to take listing photos and to access the Etsy app. YouTube has over 2 billion active users and is the second-largest search engine in the world. By starting a channel, you can reach a larger audience and increase exposure for your Etsy shop.

YouTube is a great platform to showcase your products through longer videos, unlike Instagram's and TikTok's shorter formats. You can apply the same ideas we discussed for Instagram *Reels* and TikTok clips to create engaging YouTube videos. Videos of you sourcing and shipping as well as offering tips and tricks about collecting and caring for antiques are all popular topics on YouTube. Plus, Etsy is a popular home-based business topic on YouTube, and sharing your selling journey on the site may attract a large audience, especially considering that most reselling content revolves around eBay and Poshmark, so there is less competition for an audience.

Need help starting your own YouTube channel? Check out my book, *Beginner's Guide To Starting a YouTube Channel,* which is available on Amazon!

PRO TIP: An easy way to create multiple social media posts with one single clip is to film a 60-second TikTok video. Save that video and share it on Instagram as a *Reel.* The Instagram *Reel* will post to your Instagram static feed; from there, share the *Reel* to your Instagram *Stories*. If your Instagram and Facebook pages are linked, the clip will also post to your Facebook page. And if you have a YouTube channel, you can share the clip there as a *Short.* One 60-second video will gain you maximum exposure across all of your social media platforms!

Etsy's Marketing Tools: While social media platforms such as Facebook, Instagram, Twitter, Pinterest, TikTok, and YouTube are all great ways to build your digital brand, Etsy itself offers several marketing tools to help sellers promote their products and reach new customers. Some are free, while others do cost money.

Some of the marketing tools available on Etsy include:

Shop Announcements: This free feature allows you to create a message that will be displayed on your shop's homepage and in the emails you send to your customers. You can use this section to announce your newest listings, highlight your best-selling categories, share the story behind your shop, offer special promotions and discounts, and keep the customer informed of any changes or updates to your shop.

Etsy Ads: *Etsy Ads* allow you to create targeted ads that will be displayed to potential customers who are searching for products like yours on Etsy. To **create an ad for your shop on Etsy**, go to your **Seller Dashboard** and click on the **Marketing** tab. Click on **Etsy Ads**. Choose a daily budget anywhere from $1 to $100.

I recommend starting with $5 a day and letting the ad run for at least a week to see how it performs. If you are correctly utilizing Etsy SEO and are using social media to promote your shop, you may find that Etsy Ads aren't worth the added expense. I focus on SEO and social media to drive traffic to my shop. But the only way you can know for sure is to test Etsy Ads out for yourself.

Etsy Offsite Ads: As we've discussed, this feature allows you to place ads that will be displayed on other websites and platforms, such as Facebook, Instagram, Pinterest, and Google. For sellers with less than $10,000 in yearly sales, Etsy *Offsite Ads* are an optional program one needs to opt into. However, it is mandatory and automatic for shops that sell over $10,000 a year.

Remember that you only pay for an offsite ad if it leads to a sale. You do not pay if someone clicks on the ad but does not make a purchase. So, there is no risk of opting into these ads as you aren't going to lose money. Rather, you will have the potential to make more money if the ad leads to a sale. And the more sales your shop makes, the more Etsy will push your stores in the search results, leading to more sales.

You can end your Etsy *Offsite Ads* at any time unless you are automatically enrolled due to selling over $10,000 a year. There is no way to end or opt out of *Offsite Ads* for sellers who sell over $10,000. While this may seem unfair, to be honest, if you are selling over $10,000 a year on Etsy, *Offsite Ads* should be affordable for you. Again, you only pay if the click on an ad leads to a sale, meaning you aren't risking anything. Rather, you are making a sale when you otherwise wouldn't have made one. And as long as you are pricing your items to ensure you are making a good net profit, the added fee won't cut too much into your profits.

To access the **Offside Ads** section of your account, go to your **Seller Dashboard** and click on the **Settings** tab. Then click on **Offsite Ads.**

Sales & Discounts: You can create various sales and discounts for both new and returning customers. You will find the **Sales & Discounts** section under the **Marketing** tab in your Etsy dashboard.

You can offer a **percentage off** the purchase price for a specific product or the entire order. For example, you could offer a 20% discount on all items within a certain shop section or a 20% discount on all orders over $50. Etsy automatically applies the discount for you, and the offer is shown under the thumbnail photos of your listings, which can help draw customers in.

For example, in my Etsy sticker shop, I may decide to offer 30% off any three items. That 30% discount shows up under the price of all of my listings, which entices shoppers to click through to my shop to learn more about the sale. I find that when I run a sale, my orders increase, even if customers don't end up ordering enough to score the discount. The *On Sale* verbiage is enough to draw them in. And Etsy will also show the time remaining for a sale price; so if you set it for a short time, the countdown clock can pressure shoppers to purchase before the sale ends.

The alternative to offering a percentage off is that you can instead offer a **fixed amount off** the purchase price for a specific product or the entire order. For example, you could offer a $5 discount on all products or a $20 discount on orders over $100. I haven't found this amount off option to be as effective as the percentage off option, but you should test it out to see which works best for your shop. The great thing about Etsy is that you can play around with the various options to see what works best for you.

Sale events: Etsy allows sellers to create sales events, which allow you to offer a discount on a selection of your products for a limited time. Some of the offers you can send include:

Thank you: Invite up to 200 recent customers back with a thank you offer by sending them an offer to show appreciation and encourage them to shop again. You can choose a discount amount of a percentage off or a fixed amount off. I have found this to be highly effective. I like to offer a fixed amount off, such as $10 off an order of $50.

Favorited item: You can send offers to anyone who favors one of your items. Choose a discount percentage or a fixed amount off. Note that there is no minimum order option for the *Favorited Item* offers; it applies to the single item that someone has favorited, not if they order other items from your shop. Offering a discount on an item someone has favored may be the nudge it takes for them to make the purchase!

Abandoned cart: Remind shoppers to check out by sending an offer when someone leaves an item from your shop in their cart. As with *favorited items*, you can choose a discount percentage or a fixed amount off; and there is no minimum order amount as the offer applies to a single item that someone has put into their cart. You can see what items are in people's carts by switching from your *Shop Manager* to your mail Etsy page. It's also a great way to track what items are drawing interest as you can focus on sourcing more of those products.

Run a sale: Sales are the best way to get orders, and you can lower prices for your whole shop or select categories. Many professional Etsy sellers will tell you that you should always be running sales and that your sales should be short-term for no longer than 48 hours. This is because Etsy will show shoppers a countdown clock of the remaining time in a sale, which can create a sense of urgency. These sellers typically run the same sale every two days. This can be hard to keep up with, however. I typically run sales for seven days as this is easier for me to manage.

PRO TIP: Be careful with offering any discount or exclusive offer as you don't want to mark your items down so low that you don't make a profit, or worse, loss money. The truth is that most Etsy sellers raise their prices over what the market rate is so that they can always have their items "on sale." And they often run short-term sales of 48 hours or less so that Etsy will show customers a count-down clock to encourage them to shop before the sale ends.

Is it frustrating to have to play this "sale" game to get orders? Yes. But it is a fact of the retail industry. Customers have been trained to look for discounts, meaning most people buy more items when they are on sale. Make sure you know your numbers so you can play the discount game to help you sell more items, not lose money.

Before offering any type of discount, I use an Etsy fee calculator to figure out my costs and actual net profit. There are many free Etsy fee calculators available online. My personal favorite is omniprofit.calculator.com/etsy-fee-calculator.

Create a promo code: Etsy allows shops to create a custom code to send to customers directly. You will need to enter a code name, a description of the offer, and the discount amount. You can also choose to set an expiration date and a minimum purchase amount. And you can manually end your coupon codes at any time.

Etsy does not distribute these coupon codes, however; that is something you need to do on your own. If you have a mailing list or Facebook group, you can share these special promo codes with those customers. I have a Facebook group specifically for my Etsy sticker shop and frequently create special promo codes just for members. I also only make these coupon codes available for a limited time to create a sense of urgency for people to place their orders.

Blog/Website: Creating a blog or dedicated website can be a great way to establish your brand. However, it can also add more work to your plate. I sell my antiques on eBay, Etsy, and WhatNot. I used to have a website for my reselling business, but I gave that up in favor of utilizing social media to drive traffic to my listings.

Some things to consider when deciding whether to create a website include:

- **Do you plan to publish articles discussing the items you sell?** Blogs are often seen as a research source on various topics. If you plan to only post new products and not offer any other information besides that, a website isn't worth your time as you can do the same for free on Facebook and the other social media platforms.

- **Are you looking to use your site not just as a sales channel but also as a teaching tool?** For example, if you sell glass, do you want to expand into teaching people how to identify the various antique and vintage glass makers? Or maybe you specialize in vintage dolls and want to write articles about collecting these toys.

- **Do you want to sell products only through Etsy or do you plan to eventually expand to selling on other platforms?** If you do want to eventually grow beyond Etsy, then a website could serve as a landing page for all of your links. And many web hosting services also offer the ability to add a store right on your website.

- **Do you want to utilize affiliate advertising or sell advertising on your site to earn extra money?** Google AdSense and Amazon Associates are just two of the programs that allow you to earn money by placing links on your blog. If you've even visited a blog, especially ones that feature recipes, you have likely noticed that there are more ads on those sites than information. Those sites are utilizing affiliate marketing to earn money.

If you answered "yes" to any of the above questions, then you may want to consider starting a website. However, you will need to decide whether to go with a free blogging platform or a paid website. If you decide to go the paid route, you can invest in a sophisticated system or choose a simple, low-cost one.

Yes, there are lots of decisions to make when deciding whether or not to start a website!

You can create a blog for your Etsy shop using several free platforms, such as Blogger and WordPress. It's worth noting that Google owns Blogger, which means you can apply for a *Google AdSense* account and place ads on your blog to generate extra revenue. Another popular affiliate program is *Amazon Associates,* which allows you to earn money through referral links on your website. A blog will allow you to utilize *Google AdSense, Amazon Associates*, and other affiliate programs to further monetize your online presence, drive traffic to your Etsy listings, and increase sales.

If you decide to create a paid website for your Etsy business, remember that your Etsy shop should remain the focus of your brand, with your blog or website serving as an additional tool to drive traffic to your listings. There are many low-cost website options available, such as GoDaddy.com and Wix.com, which offer not only URL registrations but also inexpensive hosting and simple website-building tools. And they also offer the ability to, for a price, sell your products directly on their sites.

As I mentioned, I no longer have a blog for my reselling business. However, because I use the pen name *Jean Lee* for both my Etsy shop and the journals I sell on Amazon, I have a website at *JeanLeePublishing.com* that I pay for through GoDaddy that serves as a landing page for both platforms. When you register a URL with GoDaddy, they will offer you add-on options such as a website. This is the option I use for my *Jean Lee* site as it is inexpensive and easy to maintain. I can easily tell people my site is at "Jean Lee Publishing dot com." From there, they can choose to click through to my *Amazon Author Page* or my Etsy shop.

Alternatively, though, I do not have a website for my name, *Ann Eckhart,* which is the name I publish my non-fiction e-commerce books (such as the one you are reading now!) under. Rather, I simply point people directly to my *Amazon Author Page*, which is where they can buy my books. Because I only have one "store" for my non-fiction books, which is my author page, I don't need a separate website. My *Amazon Author Page* is essentially my website.

Domain Name: Whether you look at selling antiques as a side hustle or as a full-time business, you want to secure the domain name for your Etsy shop. A domain name is a personal website address closely tied to your Etsy shop name. This can make it easier for customers to find and remember your website, as well as give you a professional online presence. I own several domain names for my various businesses; I make sure to always lock in a name whenever I start a new venture to ensure that I own the URLs before someone else snatches them up. I also purchase the most popular URL options, including .com, .org, and .info.

You can purchase domain names through websites like **GoDaddy.com** and link them to your Etsy shop and other online platforms. For example, I have the domain *AnnEckhart.com* that directs users directly to my *Amazon Storefront* where all my books are listed. And *JeanLeePublishing.com* takes users to a website that directs them to my Etsy shop or my Amazon page for my journal brand, both of which I have under the same pen name. I also have a domain name for eBay that points directly to my eBay store.

When thinking about registering for a domain name, it's important to consider where you want the URL to direct users. Do you want people to go to your website first, or do you want them to always go directly to your Etsy shop? Remember that a website and your social media accounts should *complement* your Etsy shop, not serve as a replacement for it. So, if you are solely selling on Etsy, you want your URL to point to your Etsy shop. And even if you are selling on multiple platforms as well as locally, you can organize all of your links on a Facebook page or using a Linktr.ee service so that users can click through to the site they want.

If you are using a free blog on a platform like Blogger, I recommend choosing a domain name that directs people directly to your Etsy shop, and keep the URL provided by Blogger for your blog as-is. Or you could choose a different domain name specifically for your blog, such as "MyEtsyShopBlog.com". For example, I use the URL *anneckhart.com* to point users directly to my *Amazon Author Page*, but the URL *jeanleepublishing.com* points directly to my GoDaddy website.

In my opinion, if you are only selling on Etsy, it's important to have a personalized URL address that points directly to your Etsy shop, as your primary focus should always be on driving sales through Etsy. A website should work to send traffic to your Etsy listings, rather than intercept it. And if Etsy is your only online selling platform, you can easily use a Facebook business page as a sort of website as you can put multiple links there, which will save you time and money over building a stand-alone site. You can add multiple links to a Facebook page, so if you sell locally at an antique mall, for instance, you can easily put that information alongside your Etsy shop on a Facebook page. In the future, if you do grow beyond Etsy or decide you want to share more information about antiques, you can easily start a website then and redirect the URL to your site at that time.

Mailing List: Creating a loyal customer base for your Etsy shop means you will have repeat customers who come back to your Etsy shop again and again because they love your products. And if you are utilizing social media, your customers may have gotten to know you on a more personal level, which also leads to strong customer loyalty. Shoppers favor brands that get to know their customers, and if you engage with your following on social media, that engagement will translate to repeat buyers.

And while social media is a great way to reach customers, to keep your most loyal buyers informed and engaged, you may want to consider setting up a mailing list that you can use to send out newsletters. Mailing lists and newsletters offer an affordable way for you to connect directly with buyers by offering giveaways, special discount codes, and a first look at new listings.

Most mailing services have free options that allow you to start collecting and growing your email lists, allowing you to upgrade to paid versions once you have reached a larger following. Some popular mailing list services include:

- AWeber
- Campaign Monitor
- Constant Contact
- Drip
- GetResponse
- Mailchimp

These services provide tools for creating and managing email campaigns, including email design templates, subscriber lists, analytics, and automation features. Many also offer integrations with other marketing and sales tools, such as e-commerce platforms and CRM software. You can create a landing page to collect email addresses; and if you sell your antiques locally, you can collect email addresses using a sign-up sheet in your vendor booth. This would be a great way to turn in-person shoppers into online customers.

PRO TIP: If you do start to collect email addresses for a mailing list, make sure you keep a file of those addresses on your computer system or backup hard drive, not only on the mailing list server. If you decide to stop using that mailing service, you will lose access to those emails. Always make sure you have a backup so you can start a new list with another service if you decide to.

Note that many blogs and website platforms also have a built-in mailing list feature. For example, my site *JeanLeePublishing.com*, which is through GoDaddy, has a feature where visitors can enter their email addresses to join my mailing list. I initially used GoDaddy's newsletter feature to send out emails. However, I now use MailChimp. I've been able to easily install a pop-up on my website that allows visitors to sign up for my MailChimp email list. And since I still have access to the email list I build directly on GoDaddy, I have simply moved those email addresses to my MailChimp account.

Remember to only send emails to individuals who have specifically opted in to receive them so that you comply with anti-spam laws and avoid annoying or alienating your customers. Send newsletters sparingly, no more than once a week. And only send newsletters when you have interesting and valuable content to share. It's better to send a monthly newsletter that is jam-packed with good content than it is to send weekly newsletters with little value.

Putting It All Together: If you're feeling overwhelmed by all the different social networking sites, marketing techniques, and advertising possibilities, take a deep breath and remember to take things one step at a time. Start with Facebook, as it is the easiest and most effective. Then expand to Twitter, Pinterest, and Instagram, as you can stick to static posts on all of them. If you feel comfortable adding videos, you can grow to include TikTok and YouTube. Or just choose one site to focus on, the one you most enjoy. Some Etsy shops only use Facebook, while others use TikTok exclusively.

When you have an Etsy shop, your primary focus should be sourcing new products and getting those items listed. Hopefully, you'll stay busy processing orders, too. Etsy SEO along with good photos are essential in creating an Etsy listing that will result in shoppers finding your items. Think of social media as a bonus step in the listing creation process, a step that comes after you have listed new items in your shop.

To promote your listings on social media, remember that you can use the "share" buttons provided by Etsy in every active listing. Simply click on an active listing and then click on the buttons for Facebook, Twitter, and Pinterest to share your listings on these platforms. As we've discussed, hashtags are incredibly useful to increase the visibility of your social media posts on Twitter, Instagram, and TikTok. Once you have connected your Etsy account to your social media networks, you can easily share your listings with just a few clicks and add a handful of relevant hashtags.

To avoid overwhelming your followers on Facebook with multiple listings at once, I recommend spreading your posts out. You can schedule posts on Facebook to space them out over the day. On Twitter and Pinterest, it is generally okay to share posts one after the other as the feeds on both platforms move much faster than on Facebook.

To promote your business on Instagram, it is important to post regularly and engage with other users. Try to post at least once a day. Instagram users enjoy personal content, so consider sharing photos of your office, new inventory, and sourcing trips along with non-business posts such as food photos from a local restaurant, beautiful nature scenes in your area, or your personal collection of antiques.

Don't forget to include three to five hashtags with each Instagram post to make it easier for potential customers to find you. Try adding videos to Instagram through *Reels* and *Stories*. Once you are comfortable creating videos, consider expanding to TikTok and even YouTube. You can add 60-second videos to YouTube as a Short.

If you have the time and resources to create and maintain a website, it can be a great way to promote the antiques you have for sale. However, remember that a website will require additional work and resources, so it's important to make sure it is worth the investment. I don't recommend a website unless you expand to selling on sites other than Etsy as social media can suffice. A mailing list requires less work and may be more effective than a website, so consider adding that option before you consider starting a blog.

Always remember that your number one goal with your business is to make money. Your priority should always be sourcing antiques to resell, creating new listings, and maximizing Etsy SEO. You may find that you do enough on Etsy alone to make sales and that you don't even need social media, although having a social media presence is expected by most customers these days. If you find you need help boosting your sales, then social media platforms are an easy, effective, and free way to advertise your Etsy shop.

CHAPTER NINE: ETSY BOOKKEEPING MADE EASY

DISCLAIMER: This chapter is for informational purposes only. You should always consult with a certified public accountant (CPA) to discuss the tax laws that apply to your business. Every state and country is different when it comes to taxes, so be sure to consult with a tax professional in your area for advice on how to manage your own Etsy bookkeeping.

Let's be honest: Buying antiques for resale is fun. Making money is fun. But dealing with taxes and bookkeeping? Not so fun. However, when you're running your own business, keeping track of your finances is an essential part of your operations. You have to know your numbers to make sure you're turning a profit, and you must report your earnings to the government come tax time.

When you sell online, there is no way to "hide" the money you earn. There is an electronic record of how much money Etsy pays you, and, if you make more than $600 in a calendar year, Etsy will issue you a 1099 form at the end of the year for you to file taxes. Uncle Sam will find you one way or the other, so don't even think of trying not to pay taxes on the money you earn on Etsy.

However, the great thing about running a business is that you can claim deductions to lower your taxes. To reduce your tax bill, you need to track your business expenses. And when you are a reseller, you have plenty of expenses. Fortunately, Etsy makes it easy to keep a record of your sales as they track these numbers for you. However, you will need to record your deductions on your own. Doing so accurately can save you hundreds is not thousands of dollars come tax time.

Etsy provides us sellers with a lot of financial information to help us keep track of our shop numbers. Specifically, Etsy breaks down seller expenses, including the fees paid to them and the cost of any ads or promotions. Etsy automatically deducts these expenses from each seller's account and deposits the remaining funds into each seller's bank account.

Every business has different expenses that come with it, but retail, which includes reselling, has a lot more than most. With an antique and vintage business, there are numerous expenses that you will want to track to maximize your deductions come tax time. So while Etsy automatically deducts their selling fees, advertising fees, and shipping costs from your balance, you still need to keep track of additional expenses on your end.

Before we discuss how to track your business expenses, let's first cover the financial information Etsy provides all sellers. You can find these details updated in real-time in your account. From your **Shop Manager** dashboard, click on **Finances** to access the following:

Payment Account: The *Payment Account* section is where you can manage your payment and deposit information. To receive payment for the items you sell, you must link your bank account to Etsy. You have the option to choose your preferred deposit schedule from daily, weekly, every other week, or monthly transfers. I choose weekly payouts so that I can count on a weekly "paycheck." But if you are buying a lot of inventory several times a week, you may want to opt for daily payouts to fund your sourcing. Many resellers source at garage sales and flea markets, and most don't accept credit cards, meaning having cash to spend is essential.

Monthly Statements: The *Monthly Statements* section is, in my opinion, the most important part of the *Finances* area. Here you can access information about your Etsy sales, fees, marketing expenses, shipping costs, and net profit. You can view your monthly statements dating back to the beginning of your selling account or narrow down the time frame to however you choose. I like to track my monthly profits from year to year to see which months I can expect more sales and to also see if my sales are growing.

Regularly monitoring your net profit will give you an idea of whether you are making money or incurring a loss. Remember, though, to keep in mind that the net profit displayed by Etsy does not include your offline expenses, such as your cost of goods, office supplies, shipping supplies, internet fees, and mileage. You will need to track these fees on your own.

QuickBooks for Etsy: For a fee, you can sync your Etsy seller account with *Intuit QuickBooks* to track your sales, expenses, and tax deductions.

TurboTax for Etsy: For a fee, you can sync your Etsy seller account with *TurboTax*, which will organize your account for taxes.

Legal & Tax Information: The *Legal & Tax Information* section is where you will enter all the necessary legal information for your Etsy shop. It is in this section that you will be able to download your 1099 form at the end of the year, which is required for tax filing purposes. If you sell more than $600 within the year, Etsy will generate a 1099 tax form for you. Note that even if you are not issued a tax form, you still must report all income to the IRS.

Fees: All selling platforms charge their sellers fees, and Etsy is no exception. As we've already discussed, the fees Etsy charges cover the costs of operating the platform and providing services to its users. These fees include a **listing fee**, a **transaction fee**, and a **payment processing fee.**

To recap from earlier in this book, Etsy charges a **listing fee** whenever a seller creates a new listing. This fee is currently $0.20 per listing and is charged at the time the listing is created. Listings are active for four months and can be renewed by the seller at the end of that period for an additional $0.20. That means you can list one item for a year for only $.60.

Etsy also charges a **transaction fee** whenever an item sells. This fee is currently 5% of the item's sale price, plus any shipping and gift wrap charges. The transaction fee is charged at the time the sale is made.

Finally, Etsy charges a **payment processing fee** whenever they process a sale. This fee varies depending on the payment method used but is typically around 3% of the total transaction amount plus a fixed fee. The payment processing fee is deducted from the seller's account at the time the payment is processed.

Expenses: All businesses can claim business-related expenses as deductions on their taxes. With an Etsy antique shop, your expenses will include:

- **Fees:** The fees charged by Etsy are automatically deducted from your account before your net profit is disbursed to you. If the fees are not specified on the tax form issued by Etsy, then you shouldn't need to report them during tax season. However, check with your CPA or tax preparer to be sure you are following the current tax laws for your area.
- **Inventory:** The biggest expense for resellers is inventory, also referred to as the "cost of goods," or "COGs" for short. Be sure to track all of the items you buy to resell. I try to use a credit card with a good points system to pay for my inventory, but if I am at a garage sale, I usually have to pay with cash. I keep a notebook handy to write down any cash I spend, and I also reconcile my credit card statement every month to note when I use my card to buy inventory.
- **Office Supplies:** Pens, paper, paperclips, printer ink, and any other office supplies you use to run your Etsy shop can all be

claimed as business expenses. I use a dedicated business credit card to pay for my business expenses, including office supplies.

- **Shipping Supplies:** Next to inventory, shipping supplies are usually the next biggest expense for Etsy antique shops. Shipping boxes, tape, shipping labels, and packing materials can all add up quickly. Just as I charge inventory and office supplies to a credit card, I also charge my shipping supplies. I only order shipping supplies from three different companies, which makes keeping track of those expenses easy.

- **Advertising & Marketing:** Etsy will automatically deduct any charges for their ads, whether they are regular ads or off-site ads. However, if you advertise on Facebook or other social media websites, you will need to track those expenses yourself. You can see your yearly Facebook ad expenses in your Facebook account. I order business card enclosures for my online business and note those expenses under *Advertising & Marketing.*

- **Home Office:** If you run your Etsy business from home, you may be able to claim a portion of your rent, utilities, and other home office expenses as a tax deduction.

- **Communications:** You can claim your internet service for your Etsy business. And if you use your smartphone for any business-related tasks, you can claim that as well.

- **Business Travel:** If you attend antique shows or other events related to your business, you can claim the cost of transportation, lodging, and meals as a deduction. And you can also claim mileage from driving around to various thrift stores, antique malls, and garage sales when out sourcing for inventory to resell.

- **Legal & Professional Fees:** This includes the cost of any legal or professional services you use in connection with your

Etsy shop, such as accounting or tax preparation services.

- **Website Services:** If you pay for a dedicated URL, standalone website, and/or a mailing list service, you can claim them as business expenses.

Tracking your Etsy business expenses: There are several ways you can track your Etsy expenses to help manage your business and prepare for tax time. Here are a few options you can consider:

- **Use Etsy's built-in invoicing and payment tools to track your income and expenses.** These tools can help you keep track of the money you have earned, the fees you have paid to Etsy, and the expenses you have incurred in running your business.
- **Use accounting software to manage your finances.** There are many different accounting software options available, and some are specifically designed for small businesses or online marketplaces like Etsy. These tools track your income and expenses, generate reports, and prepare for tax time. TurboTax is the most popular of these services.
- **Keep detailed records of your income and expenses, such as receipts, invoices, and bank statements on a computer spreadsheet or even in a notebook.** Most of your income and expenses will be recorded online on Etsy and your credit card and bank statements. This makes transferring that data to your computer or paper easy.
- **Hire a certified public accountant or professional tax preparer.** Turning to an expert to handle your financial management and tax preparation can be money well spent. In addition to filing your taxes, they can also provide expert guidance on managing your finances.

My Way: Etsy automatically deducts fees and advertising costs from my account and only pays me the remaining balance, which is displayed under **Net Profit** in my Etsy account. At the end of the year, Etsy provides me with a 1099 form that lists my net profit after all of their fees have been deducted. On my end, I only need to keep track of my deductions that occur outside of the platform, meaning I do not need to track my Etsy fees or Etsy advertising expenses.

Remember that your gross sales are your sales BEFORE any fees or expenses are taken out. On Etsy, they will show you your NET profit after they take THEIR fees and advertising costs. However, as noted earlier, there are many more expenses you can claim as deductions when it comes time to file your taxes. I note my Etsy payouts as gross sales in my bookkeeping ledger. After I account for all of my other expenses do I come to my actual net profit.

I use a basic spreadsheet to track my monthly expenses. Every month I record what I paid for web services (GoDaddy and MailChimp), advertising costs (Facebook and TikTok ads), communications expenses (internet and cell phone), inventory, office supplies, and shipping supplies. I also use an app to track my mileage.

Those are my only month-to-month Etsy business expenses. My accountant figures out how much I can claim for my home office, and he also figures out how much mileage I can claim along with any travel costs I may have had that year.

At the end of the year, I tally every category of expenses to get the year-end total for each. For example, I will add up my inventory costs for each month and enter that number into my year-end *Cost of Goods* field. Even though I have a CPA who files my taxes for me, I still provide him with these expense breakdowns so he can accurately file my returns.

At the end of January, I download my 1099 form from Etsy. I take that along with my list of year-end expenses to my accountant so he can file my taxes.

Easy!

CHAPTER TEN: HANDLING CUSTOMER SERVICE ISSUES

If you have been selling your antiques locally or at in-person events, then you likely have some good customer service experience under your belt. While local vendor fairs tend to be drama free in terms of customer issues, selling online can be different. Online, people can hide behind screen names, which makes some people think they can say whatever they want to sellers. And while the vast majority of Etsy customers are wonderful people, now and then, a difficult customer will come along that will make you question why you started your business in the first place!

The best way to deal with customer service issues is to avoid them in the first place. Having clear policies stated in your listings and in your shop will help protect you in case a customer makes a claim against you. For example, if a customer claims that they wanted their order customized, but you didn't have customization set up in the listing, then Etsy will back you if the customer files a claim.

It's not enough to just state your policies in your Etsy shop and listings, however; you need to live up to these promises on your end. As long as you follow your own policies, Etsy will take your side if a customer files a claim. But the best way to not have problems with customers is to do everything you can do to avoid issues in the first place.

Here are some ways you can be proactive in your Etsy customer service to avoid problems:

Set realistic shipping times: It's important to be upfront with customers about how long it will take for their orders to be shipped. Make sure you have enough time to properly package items and get them to your carrier. Customers favor fast shipping times, so you want to ship orders as quickly as possible. But when shipping fragile antique and vintage items such as glass and other breakables, you need to give yourself plenty of time to secure pieces to ensure they arrive intact.

I follow the "under promise and overdeliver" mantra with my reselling business by stating a longer handling time than I need. For example, I usually state that I ship orders within three business days. But in actuality, I almost always ship orders the following business day. My customers are always happy when their orders arrive faster than expected. But the longer stated time gives me a buffer in case of an emergency. It's a win-win for both my business and my buyers.

Managing customer expectations: When a customer places an Etsy order from your shop, unless you are shipping the item immediately, you may want to send them a message letting them know when their order will be shipped, and what to expect in terms of shipping times. If there are any delays or unexpected issues, let the customer know as soon as possible. While you should have your handling time clearly stated, and while Etsy will show the customer how long it will take for their item to arrive once you've shipped it, it never hurts to send your customer a quick note to reassure them that you are working on their order and when to expect it.

For me, I typically print shipping labels within an hour or two of an Etsy order coming in. Once I print a shipping label, Etsy immediately contacts the customer on my behalf to let them know their order has been processed. Etsy provides the customer with a tracking number for their order, which will only show that the package is actually in transit once the postal carrier scans it in. In these cases, there is no reason for me to contact my buyer with another message letting them know their order has shipped. Etsy has handled this communication for me, and I am not going to bother the buyer with a message stating the same thing.

However, if for some reason I wasn't able to ship the following business day (and remember, business days are Monday through Friday, not weekends or federal holidays), then I would perhaps send the customer a message. As an example, let's say there is a storm that knocks out power in my area for a day, delaying my ability to print a shipping label until 36 hours after the customer placed their order. In this instance, even though I am still within my three-day shipping window, I may send a message stating, *Thank you for your order! We are currently packaging up your item and will ship it out on Wednesday. Once it is in the hands of the postal service, they will scan it in and your tracking number will upload to your account. Thank you again for your business!*

As you can see, I didn't mention the power outage or make excuses for the delay in printing the shipping label. Instead, I simply reassured the customer that their order has been received, that it is being processed, and that tracking will upload soon. This message lets the customer know that while they haven't yet gotten a notification of their order being shipped that I as the seller am fully aware of their order and am working on it.

PRO TIP: In cases where an entire region is being affected by a natural disaster, such as a hurricane or tornado, Etsy will usually issue a notice to seller and buyers about a potential delay in shipping. If you live in an area where severe weather is common, consider putting your shop on vacation when there is a warning in your area. This will prevent new orders from coming in until you turn your vacation settings off.

Handling lost or damaged shipments: Unfortunately, packages can sometimes be lost or damaged in transit. I have been selling online since 2005 on all of the major platforms, and the vast majority of packages arrived with no issues. However, when a package has been lost or arrives at the customer's location damaged, it's important to immediately address the situation.

When a customer contacts you to report that their package has not arrived, the first step is to ask the customer to wait for a couple of days. Sometimes, packages are delivered to a neighbor's house, or they may have been scanned as delivered but still be on the mail truck. Often, it turns out that someone else in the household has brought the delivery inside but didn't tell the actual customer about the package. I always encourage my buyers to wait for two days to see if their package turns up, and they usually do.

However, if a buyer's package still hasn't arrived after two or three days after tracking says it was delivered, kindly direct your customer to contact their local Post Office or speak to their mail carrier. Explain to your buyer that the package is in the hands of the USPS in their area and that you have no control over it once it leaves your hands. But even though you can't do anything on your end, it is important to maintain a professional and helpful attitude, as the customer will likely be frustrated. Let them know you are on their side and that will help them resolve the issue.

If there is no resolution from the Post Office, you then need to direct your customer to file a claim with Etsy. Since you purchased the shipping label through Etsy and the tracking information shows the package as delivered, Etsy will take responsibility for the missing package and refund the customer, without any financial loss on your part. This is part of Etsy's protection program for both buyers and sellers, which is one of the many benefits of selling on Etsy.

If a package arrives to your customer with visible damage to the shipping box, you may be able to put in a claim with USPS. However, it may be easier for you to refund the customer directly and then seek a refund directly from the Post Office as asking the customer to file a claim can often be confusing and time-consuming. Note that you will need photographic evidence of the damaged box to file a claim, so anytime a customer contacts you about damage, immediately direct them to take a photo and send it to you through Etsy's messaging system. Almost everyone these days has a smartphone with a camera, so there is no reason customers can't send you pictures.

If an order arrives with the product inside damaged, but there is no damage to the shipping box, it may be harder to prove that it was the Post Office's fault, and filing a claim with USPS may not be successful. In this case, you may need to absorb the cost of the refund. If an item arrives damaged, I issue the buyer a refund and tell them to keep the item. Asking the customer to return the damaged product is an inconvenience to them. And as a seller, having the item shipped back to you means that in addition to issuing a refund for the original order, you then have to pay for the return postage. Unless it is a high-dollar item, it is easier and cheaper to just issue a full refund and allow the customer to keep the product, which they can repair, donate, or throw away.

To avoid products breaking during shipment, it's essential to overpack orders to ensure the item has the best chance of arriving intact. If you are getting multiple reports of products breaking during shipment, it's a lesson that you need to do a better job packing your orders.

PRO TIP: Bubble wrap, packing peanuts, and packing paper are essential for shipping breakables. After I package an order, I shake the box. If I hear or feel anything moving around inside the package, I open it back up and add more packing materials.

Responding to messages on Etsy: While selling online means you often have little to no direct interaction with customers, you will on occasion get messages through Etsy regarding your products and orders. It's important to respond to these messages as quickly as possible as Etsy rates your response time. If you are slow to answer messages, it will reflect poorly on your shop. I have the Etsy app installed on my phone so that I can respond to messages quickly no matter where I am, even if it is just to tell the person messaging me that I am away from the office but will answer their question when I get back.

Every seller eventually has a customer message them upset that their order hasn't arrived, they were sent the wrong item, or that the item itself was damaged during shipment. While it can be difficult to deal with an upset buyer, it's important to remain calm and professional. When a customer is angry, try to respond with empathy and understanding. For example, you might say, "I am so sorry to hear that there's an issue with your order. Let me see what I can do to help."

If the customer claims that an item arrived damaged, ask them to send photos of the product. Again, almost everyone these days has a smartphone, which makes it easy for the buyer to take a photo and sent it to you through Etsy's messaging system. If the photos confirm that the item was damaged during shipping, apologize, and offer a full refund. A customer who balks at providing a photo may be trying to make a false claim about the item being damaged. Stand firm about them providing a picture as Etsy will also back you up in this situation. No photo, no refund!

In cases where the mistake was the buyer's fault, such as entering the wrong shipping address or making an error when ordering, it's important to explain politely but firmly that you are unable to refund the purchase due to your shop policies and the fact that the mistake wasn't your fault. If the customers persist, encourage them to file a claim with Etsy. Etsy should side with you and decline the return. Again, by remaining calm, expressing empathy, and then redirecting the customer to file a direct claim with Etsy, you help remove yourself from the situation and allow Etsy to take over.

Only use Etsy's messaging system: I do not give out my email or phone number to customers as I want to make sure all communications go through Etsy. Etsy can access messages, so if you are being harassed or threatened by an upset customer, you will have the messages as evidence. However, if the communication happens outside of Etsy, you lose your *Seller Protection*. If a customer somehow gets my email, I simply avoid their messages. Again, any communication outside of Etsy cancels out your *Seller Protection*, so resist the urge to respond to emails and only engage with messages sent through Etsy.

Managing customer expectations: As I've mentioned previously, I like to "under promise and over deliver" when it comes to my online shops. While I usually ship orders the following business day, I set my handling times for two to three days to give me a buffer. If I can ship earlier, the customer is happy. I also, when possible, upgrade shipping. While I may list an item with *Ground* as the shipping method, I usually upgrade the order to ship via *Priority Mail*. Not only is *Priority* faster, but I can also use a free USPS box.

Don't oversell: I also make sure to not oversell my products, meaning I don't make claims that simply aren't true. I state the facts of the product, such as the size and condition. Antiques are secondhand, used items; it's rare to find an antique or vintage piece in brand-new condition. Even if an item, such as a vintage toy, is unused in its original box, the box itself almost always shows some wear due to age and storage.

Avoid terms such as "brand new condition," "perfect condition," "like new," or "mint," as the fact that the item is 20 years or older means that it isn't brand new. It was likely sold in a store and then kept by at least one owner before you purchased it to resell on Etsy. If I am selling an item that looks to be in perfect condition, I still only state the facts, which are that it is in good, clean condition with no flaws.

Pictures go a long way toward managing customer expectations. I take upclose, clear photos to ensure the products I'm selling are shown as-is. I take photos of items on every side, including the top and bottom. I try to provide enough pictures so that the customer is seeing the item from all angles, the same way they would if they were buying the item in person. I take close-up shots of maker marks and brand labels if there are any. And I take pictures of any flaws the item may have, no matter how small. Antique buyers know vintage items aren't going to be perfect and will buy items with tiny imperfections as long as you disclose them upfront.

I also work to offer fair pricing and shipping charges. By using a digital postal scale, I can list my items with accurate shipping weights. I use calculated shipping on most items so that the buyer pays the exact postage amount based on the weight of the order and the zip code it is shipping to.

Finally, I don't claim any of the items I sell will change someone's life or that they are the best products of their kind on the market. While national name brands may be able to make such bold claims, I, as a small business owner, cannot. I don't promise same-day shipping when I know I will need a day or two to process a sale. I don't list a vintage ceramic figurine as "like new" when it has a small flea bite chip on the bottom or some mild paint fade on the back. And I don't claim the item is the best available, or that my shop is better than another seller's store.

Dealing with difficult buyers: Sometimes, despite your best efforts, you simply cannot make a buyer happy and they, for reasons that seem unfair, leave you negative feedback. If you find that someone has left you negative feedback on Etsy, it's important to remain calm and professional. Lashing out at the buyer on Etsy or social media isn't going to reflect well on you or your shop.

First off, realize that most businesses, even small online shops, will eventually receive negative feedback. I've been selling online since 2005 and have had a handful of negatives over the years. Fortunately, when you run a busy shop, a negative will quickly get buried by (hopefully) the positive reviews. Most buyers understand this and won't let one negative review stop them from buying from you, especially if you have lots of positive reviews to back up your shop.

Sometimes a buyer will leave a negative review without first contacting you, but usually, a negative is left by a customer after they feel you haven't resolved their complaint. Remember that when dealing with a difficult buyer, it's important to listen carefully to their concerns and try to understand their perspective. Even if you disagree with their complaints, showing empathy and understanding can go a long way toward defusing a tense situation.

I try to remember that many buyers have had negative experiences dealing with online sellers, especially those on eBay, Etsy, and Poshmark; and, expecting a fight, they come out swinging. By gently letting them know you hear their concerns and are going to help them, you can often diffuse the situation. Most people just want to be heard. By responding with a simple statement such as, "I'm so sorry you are unhappy with your order. Let's see if we can work to find a solution," can de-escalate the situation.

Asking what the customer would like you to do to resolve the situation may result in them asking for a small partial refund. For example, I once had a customer who was upset that one small ornament in a lot they had ordered arrived broken. They sent me a very harsh message, but rather than respond in anger, I took a deep breath, apologized, and asked if I could offer a small partial refund to make up for the broken item. The customer asked for a $5 refund, which I happily gave. The customer was so happy that I had worked to resolve the issue quickly that they apologized for their original tone and left me positive feedback. Sure, I was out $5; but it was a small price to pay to make a customer happy and avoid a negative.

However, if you can't calm down a customer and they escalate to threatening you, you need to take action to protect yourself and your shop. Here are some steps you can take to have Etsy intervene on your behalf:

1. **Contact Etsy:** You can report problematic buyers to Etsy by clicking on the **Contact Etsy Support** link on the Etsy homepage. You can also contact Etsy through the **Help** section of your shop dashboard. Look for these links at the bottom of every Etsy page when using the site on a desktop computer.

2. **Provide evidence:** When reporting a buyer, be sure to provide evidence of their threatening behavior. Etsy has access to the messaging system, so they will be able to see any messages someone has sent you along with messages you have sent. This is why you must remain professional in your responses as Etsy will see that you aren't the one instigating the problem. If a customer has sent you direct email messages, do not respond to them but instead take screenshots of those emails to forward to Etsy.

3. **Flag the conversation:** If someone on Etsy is sending you inappropriate or abusive messages through Etsy's messaging system, do not reply to the person but rather flag the conversation. This will alert Etsy to the situation and may lead to the buyer's account being suspended or banned. Either way, the situation will be in Etsy's hands, not yours.

Etsy takes reports of threatening or abusive behavior very seriously and has policies in place to protect sellers from harassment. Don't escalate a bad situation by continuing to engage with an abusive buyer as you could then be seen as being equally threatening. By acting immediately by reporting the buyer's behavior to Etsy directly, you will help protect both yourself and your business.

Dealing with negative feedback: If you sell online long enough, you are bound to receive negative feedback. If you are doing a robust business, these negatives, while upsetting, will soon fall off, drowned out by the positive feedback scores from other customers.

Regardless, in situations where the buyer leaves you with negative feedback, it's important to remain calm. If the customer never reached out to you regarding their order, contact them through Etsy's messaging system, let them know you saw their feedback, and apologize for any issues they experienced. Avoid the urge to lash out and instead remain professional. If they are open to a resolution, ask them what you can do to have them retract their negative feedback. You may find that they are open to a partial refund or a return. If you don't normally accept returns, you may consider them in special cases if it means negative feedback is retracted.

Sometimes buyers forget that there is a real person on the other end of the computer and don't consider contacting a seller with a problem. You can often not only defuse a situation but completely turn it around by showing compassion and empathy to the buyer.

Remember that dealing with difficult buyers is a part of running a business and that it's impossible to please everyone all of the time. I don't know of any Etsy seller who has never gotten negative feedback. It happens. Try to move past it and focus on the other orders you have to process. Eventually, the one negative feedback will be buried by the positive ones you get.

Issuing refunds: If you made a mistake with an order, you need to take responsibility for it and refund the customer immediately. I prefer to issue a refund and allow the buyer to keep the item rather than have them return the item. My error has already caused a problem for my customer; I don't want to make them take the time to repackage and ship back the defective product, especially since I have to pay for the return postage. Losses happen in business; I'd rather issue a refund and move forward with my business than dwell on one sale.

Here's a step-by-step guide on how to issue a refund to a customer on Etsy:

1. Go to your Etsy shop dashboard
2. Click on **Orders & Shipping**
3. Find the order
4. Click on **Issue a refund**
5. Choose the refund amount
6. Choose the reason for the refund
7. Add a message to the buyer (optional)
8. Click **Review refund**
9. Click **Issue refund**

Once you have issued the refund, Etsy will process the refund and notify the buyer. The refund will typically be issued back to the original payment method used by the buyer. It is important to note that Etsy may withhold payment for the refunded amount from your shop payment account, depending on your payment processing settings and the timing of the refund. For example, if you have $50 in your pending Etsy balance but have to issue a refund of $55, Etsy will charge the $5 overage to the credit card you have on file.

Remember that you not only have to refund the cost of the item but the shipping, too. This is a hard pill to swallow, especially when it first happens to you. But try not to dwell on it. Again, the occasional refund is part of running a business. Depending on the issue, Etsy may or may not refund you the fees from the sale.

Etsy Seller Protection: Selling on Etsy automatically enrolls you in their *Seller Protection* program, which is designed to help protect sellers on the platform from certain types of fraudulent activities, including payment disputes, cases of unauthorized transactions, and claims of non-delivery of items. The policy includes the following measures:

1. **Payment protection:** Etsy provides payment protection for sellers who use *Etsy Payments* to process their transactions. This means that if a buyer files a payment dispute, Etsy will investigate and work to resolve the issue, and will cover any eligible losses incurred by the seller up to the full value of the transaction.

2. **Seller protection cases:** If a buyer opens a case against a seller for non-delivery, the seller can provide proof of shipment or delivery to dispute the claim. If the seller can provide proof, the case will be closed in the seller's favor, and the seller will not be responsible for refunding the buyer. This is why you want to buy all of your shipping labels through Etsy and not on a third-party platform. If you purchase postage on another site, you will cancel your seller protection.

3. **Seller protection for unauthorized transactions:** If a seller receives an unauthorized transaction, Etsy will investigate and work to resolve the issue, and will cover any eligible losses incurred by the seller up to the full value of the transaction. This happens very rarely, and when it does, Etsy has usually stopped the sale before it makes it into the seller's dashboard.

Contacting Etsy Seller Support: As an Etsy seller, there are several ways to reach out to Etsy for help:

1. **Contact Etsy's customer support team:** You can contact Etsy's customer support team by visiting the **Etsy Help Center**, which is located at the bottom of every Etsy page and clicking on the **Contact support** button. From there, you can choose the topic that best matches your issue and fill out a support request form. Etsy's support team will then respond to your request via email.

2. **Use Etsy's Seller Help Center:** Etsy's *Seller Help Center* is a comprehensive resource that provides answers to many common questions and issues that sellers may encounter. You can browse the help center's articles and guides to find information on topics such as setting up your shop, managing your orders, and resolving disputes.

3. **Join the Etsy Community:** The *Etsy Community* is a forum where sellers can connect with each other and share advice and support. You can ask questions and get advice from other sellers who may have experienced similar issues or challenges. Or you can just lurk and pick up information without posting yourself.

4. **Follow Etsy's social media channels:** Etsy frequently shares updates and announcements on its social media channels, including Twitter, Facebook, and Instagram. Following their profiles on social media can help you stay up-to-date on changes to Etsy's policies and procedures, as well as any issues or outages that may affect your shop.

PRO TIP: If, for some reason, you aren't getting a response from Etsy through their website, you can message them through social media, specifically Facebook. This will get you talking to a live person who may be able to help you faster.

Regardless of how you choose to reach out to Etsy for help, it's important to be professional and specific about your issue or question.

Make sure you provide all relevant facts and documentation to support your request. Etsy's customer support team is generally very responsive and helpful, so don't hesitate to reach out if you need assistance. Treat the team with the respect you hope that customers treat you and refrain from badgering or threats, both of which could result in your account being terminated.

Etsy Buyer Protection: Just as sellers are offered protection in certain circumstances, so are Etsy buyers. As a seller, you must understand these policies just so that you know where your customers would stand in case an issue arises. Etsy offers several buyer protections to help ensure that buyers have a positive experience when shopping on the platform. Some of these protections include:

1. **Buyer Protection Case:** If a buyer has an issue with an order, they can open a *Buyer Protection Case* within the designated timeframe to seek resolution with the seller. The buyer protection case is designed to help buyers and sellers work together to resolve issues such as non-delivery, damaged items, or items that do not match the description provided by the seller.

2. **Refund Policy:** Etsy's refund policy requires sellers to accept returns and issue refunds for items that are not as described, defective, or arrive damaged, regardless of whether or not their shop policies accept returns. Buyers have 180 days to file a refund request from the date of the purchase.

3. **Etsy's Payment Processing System:** Etsy's payment processing system provides additional protection for buyers by keeping their payment information secure and encrypted. Buyers can use various payment methods, including credit cards, debit cards, and PayPal, to make purchases on the platform. Sellers never see what payment a customer uses as Etsy handles all payments themselves.

4. **Reviews & Ratings:** Etsy's review system allows buyers to leave feedback on their purchases, including ratings and reviews of the product and the seller. This helps other buyers make informed decisions and encourages sellers to maintain high standards of quality and customer service. The ability for customers to leave public feedback is one more reason why you want to try and avoid issues in the first place.

Contacting Etsy Buyer Support: As a buyer on Etsy, there are several ways to reach out to Etsy for help:

1. **Contact Etsy's customer support team:** Just as sellers can contact Etsy's seller support team, customers can contact Etsy's customer support team by visiting the **Etsy Help Center** at the bottom of any Etsy page and clicking on the **Contact support** button. From there, they can choose the topic that best matches their issue and fill out a support request form. Etsy's support team will then respond via email.

2. **Use Etsy's Buyer Help Center:** Etsy's *Buyer Help Center* is a comprehensive resource that provides answers to many common questions and issues that buyers may encounter. Shoppers can browse the help center's articles and guides to find information on topics such as making purchases, tracking orders, and resolving disputes.

3. **Reach out to the seller:** If a customer has an issue with an order, their first step is typically to reach out to the seller directly to try to resolve the issue. Buyers can do this by clicking on the *Contact* option in their order history.

When I talk to people about my online selling journey and dealing with customer service issues, I always joke that 99.9% of buyers are amazing. It's the .1% who make things difficult. Since I started selling online in 2005, I can count on one hand how many difficult buyers I've dealt with. That is because I do my best to prevent customer complaints from happening in the first place by making sure my listings and policies are clear and that I ship orders quickly. I answer messages within an hour of them coming in. And I work hard to make things right when I make a mistake. As I've already mentioned, my motto has always been to **under promise and over deliver.** Adopt the same mentality and you, too, can prevent most Etsy customer service issues from occurring in the first place.

The *Golden Rule* applies in life and business: Treat others the way you want to be treated. And that includes dealing with your Etsy buyers!

CHAPTER ELEVEN: GROWING YOUR ANTIQUE BUSINESS

Hopefully, this book has given you all of the tools and resources you need to start selling vintage items on Etsy. Some online antique dealers only sell on Etsy, while others expand their business by selling on sites such as eBay, Poshmark, Mercari, and WhatNot. And some resellers continue to sell their items in antique malls, at flea markets, and even in their own shops.

While Etsy is a great place to sell antiques, it isn't the only place. This chapter will discuss other platforms to sell on as well as opportunities to grow your business locally.

First, however, I want to reiterate the fact that choosing to only sell antiques on Etsy is perfectly fine. Expanding to other websites takes time. Not only does it take time to learn other platforms, but selling on multiple sites means you will need to source and list more as well as closely monitor items that are cross-posted to two or more sites. If you listed a piece of vintage glass on Etsy, eBay, Mercari, and WhatNot and it sells overnight on both Etsy and eBay, you will have to cancel one of the sales, which can hurt your account standings and anger customers.

Cross-posting is for full-time sellers who have a handle on their inventory and are always monitoring their shops. However, if you do want to expand to other online platforms, you have options. First, let's break down the pros and cons of expanding your business beyond Etsy:

PROS:

1. **Increased revenue:** Selling on more platforms means that you will reach more customers and potentially make more money. While Etsy has a large customer base, other websites

get a lot more traffic, including eBay, which is the number three selling platform in America behind Amazon and Walmart.

2. **Diversification:** Selling on multiple platforms can help diversify your income streams and reduce your reliance on one platform. If you inadvertently (or deliberately) violate Etsy's rules, you could lose your account. Having accounts on other sites would mean you have backup places to sell. Of course, there are many things you can do to prevent this, but if you are a full-time antique dealer, having backup platforms is comforting "just in case."

3. **Branding:** Creating your own online store or selling on multiple platforms can help you build a more recognizable brand and increase your visibility, especially if you specialize in a particular era or aesthetic.

4. **Experimentation:** If you have built an Etsy shop based around one category, selling on other platforms can allow you to expand your offerings. Note that you can also accomplish this by opening up a second (or third or fourth) Etsy shop, which we will discuss shortly. Etsy's algorithm likes shops to have very specific niches, which makes adding new categories challenging. But other websites don't have the same SEO structure as Etsy, making it easier to flesh out your brand to multiple products under one site.

CONS:

1. **Learning curve:** Selling on multiple platforms requires you to learn new systems and processes, which can be time-consuming and challenging. Every platform has its own listing forms, payment processing system, and shipping options. Managing Etsy alone is a lot; managing several others may be too much, especially when you are selling hard

goods that you are personally sourcing. You want to spend the majority of your time sourcing, listing, and shipping, not struggling to manage several different websites, especially if the vast majority of your sales are coming from one or two platforms. If you are making good money selling on Etsy and eBay, you may not need to bother with cross-posting to Poshmark, Mercari, or other sites.

2. **Increased workload:** Expanding your business beyond Etsy may require you to handle more orders, which may become too overwhelming for you to fulfill on your own. You may need to hire help to run your business, which will cut into your profits. And having help means you will have to trust those people to meet your standards.

3. **More marketing:** Etsy SEO allows sellers to maximize the visibility of their listings both on Etsy and off. If you expand to other websites, you will need to learn new SEO strategies as well as increase your social media marketing efforts. And the more you spend on marketing, the less time you have to source, list, and ship. While other sites may have more traffic, they may not have as many antique shoppers, making it more challenging to bring in buyers for your products. Poshmark, for example, is mainly known for selling trendy clothing. It may not be worth your time to list your antiques there when you could instead focus on sites such as Etsy and eBay.

4. **Expansion stress:** Growing your business may require you to expand your workspace and hire employees. Renting office space and dealing with payroll may be more stressful than you want to take on. If you are busy enough selling your antiques locally and on Etsy, and if you want to stay a one-person operation, expanding to other platforms may not be feasible nor desirable. And that's okay! As long as you are happy with your profits, it's perfectly fine to only sell on one or two

platforms.

Opening a Second Etsy Shop: As you can see, expanding your business beyond Etsy has its benefits and its downfalls. If you are simply wanting to add more products to your offerings beyond the category you are currently selling in, the answer may be to not sell outside of Etsy but rather to open a second Etsy shop. You can have multiple Etsy shops, you just need to sign up for different accounts, which means you need to use different email addresses. You can easily get a second email address through Google using their Gmail service.

To open a second Etsy account and therefore a new Etsy shop, simply repeat the process we covered earlier in this book. Again, you will need a different email address from your first account.

Etsy allows sellers to have multiple shops, but there are some restrictions. For example, you can't have two shops selling the same items, and you can't use a second shop to get around Etsy's rules or policies. You also have to list all of your shops in the public profile section of each of your Etsy accounts. Even though you need a different email to start a second Etsy shop, you can use the same banking information as you do for your first shop. You will also use the sale taxpayer ID information.

PRO TIP: Note that sometimes new shops are automatically flagged by Etsy's automation "bot" system, which is set up to thwart bogus accounts. If this happens to you, you will receive an email explaining your new shop has been closed. But don't panic! You will simply need to contact Etsy to let them know that you indeed started a second Etsy account as you are opening a second shop. They will ask you to confirm your information. It may take a few days, but Etsy will eventually approve your new account for your new shop.

When would opening a second Etsy shop make sense? It is only beneficial if you specialize in products that are in completely different categories. Let's say your first shop is exclusively filled with retro kitschy collectibles. But you also have a large inventory of vintage clothing. These two products are in different categories, target different customers, and would have vastly different shipping profiles. In this example, opening a second shop for vintage clothing may make sense.

However, let's say you, like most resellers, sell a wide variety of antiques from different eras and in different styles. Most antique stores are a hodge podge of various products, and it's expected that an Etsy antique shop will be the same. Unless you specialize in two radically different products, having two shops would simply be more work than necessary.

Facebook Marketplace: If you've been selling your antiques locally, you may have already experimented with selling through *Facebook Marketplace*. Facebook users can post items for sale for local pick up or shipping. There are no fees involved for local pick-up items, but if you offer to ship, there may be fees. These vary, depending on the promotions the platform runs for sellers. Facebook handles the payment and shipping labels for orders, which is a benefit.

However, if you want to offer local pickup, you'll need to implement a payment system for customers. Most sellers use PayPal, Venmo, or CashApp, but some also accept cash or checks.

The biggest problem with offering local pickup on *Facebook Marketplace* is meeting people in person. Facebook is notorious for buyers reaching out to sellers, expressing interest in a product, and then disappearing before completing the sale. Or they may consistently reschedule pick-up times and locations. However, if you are patient and available for arranging pickup times, *Facebook Marketplace* can be a great way to expand your business, especially if you implement an immediate payment system so that people can't flake on you.

eBay: eBay is the third largest online marketplace in America, behind Amazon and Walmart. And it is, alongside Etsy, the most popular place to sell antiques. The difference between the two sites is minimal in terms of the user experience, both for the seller and the shopper. Listing on eBay is similar to listing on Etsy, and the shipping processes are equally similar. And just as Etsy handles all of the back-end logistics for sellers, so does eBay, including the collection and remittance of sales tax.

eBay has also been around longer and boosts a larger user base over Etsy. So why not just sell your antiques on eBay and forgo Etsy altogether? The truth is that many sellers only sell their antiques on eBay. However, the edge that Etsy has over eBay in terms of the vintage market is that Etsy shoppers are drawn to the higher quality aesthetic of Etsy shops over eBay stores. eBay has a very basic, streamlined look. Its no-frills layout attracts buyers looking for deals, whereas Etsy's more artistic layout gives customers the feel of walking into a well-laid-out antique store.

For many sellers, however, it comes down to cost. It is simply cheaper, on the surface, to list items for sale on Etsy over eBay. On Etsy, you can list one item for four months at a cost of only $.20, meaning you only pay $.60 to list an item for a year on Etsy. Also, the only store option Etsy offers is its $10-a-month Etsy Plus subscription.

Compare that with eBay, where, unless you have a store, you have to pay monthly for each of your listings. However, Ebay offers several different store subscription levels that include listings. An *eBay Starter Store* costs $5 per month and includes 250 listings. Other store subscriptions include more listings along with other benefits.

eBay also has millions of more shoppers than Etsy. If you are looking to move items quickly and are okay with perhaps not getting top dollar for your antiques, eBay is a great choice. The volume of sales you can make on eBay will often eclipse the dollar amount you can make on Etsy when all is said and done.

I like to think of the differences between Etsy and eBay as such: Etsy is like a beautiful antique store where the owner has carefully cultivated their inventory and displays. eBay is like a flea market where you have different vendor booths, each with a hodge podge of items available for sale. Neither is better, just different.

And if you want to take your antique business to the next level, expanding to eBay is the most logical step. I recommend that you start with items that have been sitting on Etsy for over four months. If an item hasn't sold after it has been listed on Etsy for that long, consider cross-posting it to eBay. eBay offers sellers the ability to enable *Best Offer* on their listings, allowing interested buyers to send offers. This alone can help move products more quickly versus Etsy, which doesn't have a *Best Offer* feature.

If you want to learn more about selling on eBay, check out my book *Beginner's Guide To Selling On eBay*, which walks you step by step through the entire process of listing, shipping, and handling customer service issues.

Poshmark: Poshmark is a platform primarily focused on fashion, accessories, and beauty items. While you may be able to sell some vintage items on Poshmark, it's not necessarily the best platform for selling antiques. Poshmark is designed for selling new or gently used clothing, but they do have a home décor section as well as categories for jewelry. You can also sell vintage clothing on Poshmark. As I recommended in the eBay section, if you have an item that has been sitting on Etsy for a while and there is a Poshmark category for it, consider cross-posting it there just to see if you get any interest.

The nice thing about selling on Poshmark is that there are no fees to list items for sale there. You only pay fees when an item sells. Poshmark handles payment processing, tax collection, and shipping labels, depositing the remaining profits into your account. So, like Etsy and eBay, the backend work is handled for you.

Poshmark sellers are very active on social media, especially Instagram and YouTube. By utilizing those two platforms, you can connect with other Poshmark sellers and grow your following on the site. And since there aren't as many vintage sellers on Poshmark as are on Etsy or eBay, there is less competition there.

Mercari: Mercari is an e-commerce platform that is similar to eBay in that it allows people to sell a wide variety of items, both new and secondhand. Vintage toys from the '80s and '90s are especially popular on Mercari. And while Mercari doesn't have as large a user base as eBay, it is very user-friendly, making it easy to list and ship items through the site. Mercari also handles all payments, sales tax, and shipping processing, just as Etsy, eBay, and Poshmark do.

Sellers can list items for sale on Mercari for free, only paying fees when a product sells. The fee is lower than those of Etsy, eBay, and Poshmark; however, the customer base is much smaller than those platforms. Additionally, since customers mainly shop on Mercari for rock-bottom deals, it may not be the best place to sell higher-priced antiques. However, if you have lower-priced items or want to liquidate excess inventory, not having to pay any listing fees is an advantage as your listings remain on Mercari's site for free until they sell.

WhatNot: WhatNot is a relatively new e-commerce platform that initially started as a live auction site for sellers of Funko collectibles, but has since expanded to include numerous categories, including the *Antiques, Vintage & Ephemera* category with the subcategories of *Vintage Décor, Antiques, Ephemera & Postcards*, and *Stamps*.

Another category is *Estate Sales & Storage Units* with the subcategories of *Estate Sales, Storage Unit Finds,* and *Garage Sales.* There are vintage categories for women's clothing, men's clothing, jewelry, and books. And finally, sports cards, Disneyana, and toys are also places to sell vintage items under.

Sellers can use WhatNot in two ways: live-streaming auctions and buy-it-now listings. Live streaming allows sellers to go live on the app to showcase their products in real-time, enabling buyers to ask questions and interact with the seller, creating a more personalized shopping experience. While most sellers run auctions, you can also sell items at a fixed price during a live sale. Additionally, sellers can list items in the *WhatNot Marketplace* section, which gives sellers a sort of storefront to list products outside of a live sale.

The live-streaming feature provides a unique opportunity for sellers to showcase their items and engage with potential buyers. However, as a newer platform, the user base isn't as large as other online marketplaces, so it's important to research the platform and its audience before deciding whether to sell on WhatNot or another platform.

I recommend that before you consider selling on WhatNot that you first become a WhatNot buyer. There are antique sellers live day and night who you can watch and learn from. WhatNot can be a great place to source antiques to resell on other platforms, too. Look for shows that don't have a large audience for the possibility of scoring deals on vintage collectibles you can sell for top dollar on Etsy.

WhatNot's fees are relatively low, and, as with the other sites we've discussed, the platform handles payment processing, tax collection, and shipping labels. The listing process is simple, straightforward, and user-friendly. You only need to enter a short title and shipping weight to list an item at auction or fixed price. You don't even need to upload a photo for an auction, although it is advisable to do so.

Despite being a relatively new platform, WhatNot is growing every day. WhatNot is often described as a social media platform with a selling element. Successful WhatNot sellers not only bring good merchandise to their sales but also run entertaining shows, often implementing giveaways and games to engage buyers.

To learn more about selling on WhatNot, check out my book, *Beginner's Guide To WhatNot,* which teaches you how to buy and sell on the app.

Shopify: For sellers who want to start their own website, Shopify is often the go-to choice. It provides a powerful and customizable platform for selling your products with a user-friendly interface and a variety of features that other platforms don't offer.

One of the main advantages of Shopify is its scalability. It's able to handle stores of all sizes, making it a good choice for small businesses and larger enterprises alike. With a range of pricing plans to choose from, Shopify can also be customized to fit a variety of needs and budgets.

However, unlike other selling platforms such as Etsy, eBay, Poshmark, Mercari, WhatNot, and Facebook Marketplace, sellers on Shopify need to implement their own payment processing, sales tax collection, and shipping services. This means that sellers need to figure out how to accept payments, collect and remit sales tax for the American states or countries that require it, and incorporate a way to print shipping labels on their own. For many small businesses, especially sole proprietors, this can be overwhelming and time-consuming.

To address the needs of sellers, Shopify offers a variety of payment processing options, including Shopify Payments, PayPal, and other third-party payment gateways. Additionally, Shopify offers tools and integrations for sales tax calculation and shipping label printing to help streamline the process. However, these services vary depending on your location and still require you to set up these third-party providers yourself to integrate them into Shopify.

While having your own dedicated website does give you complete control over your brand, I know many sellers who opened a Shopify store only to eventually close it and return to Etsy and other platforms that handle the back-end processes of running an e-commerce business. The collection and remittance of the sales tax alone is enough for many sellers, including myself, to stick with the established websites that handle those services.

I personally only think a Shopify store for antique sellers is only worth it if you sell collectibles under one brand, not a wide variety of different products under several categories. For example, some sellers have Shopify stores where they only sell vintage Department 56 collectibles. They have thousands of Department 56 items and are known for specializing in that brand. For them, a dedicated website makes sense as they have established a specialty that collectors can trust. Compare that to most antique dealers who may have some vintage Department 56 pieces alongside antique glass, retro toys, and ephemera for sale.

Expand Locally: If expanding to other online selling platforms seems like too much, you can still grow your antique business locally by seeking out antique malls and vendor shows in your area. Antique malls rent booth space to dealers and usually take a percentage of sales. Most require that you set up your booth with shelving and displays.

Also, look for antique shows within a reasonable driving distance from where you live. Antique shows can be profitable if you know the audience and have desirable items priced to sell. Also, some farmers markets allow antique dealers. These in-person events may not be the most profitable place to sell your items, but they offer you a chance to promote your Etsy shop by handing out business cards or flyers. For example, if you have a booth at a vendor show, consider printing out flyers with a coupon for your Etsy shop.

Finally, don't underestimate the power of networking and word-of-mouth marketing. Consider attending local business events and networking groups to connect with other entrepreneurs and potential customers. These connections can also be a fantastic way to source antiques as they can lead to bulk buys.

ANN ECKHART

CONCLUSION

Whether you have been an antique dealer for decades or are just now discovering the career (and profitability) of reselling vintage collectibles, I hope this book has given you all of the tools you need to start selling on Etsy. If this is your first time selling online, remember to take things slow. Start with listing a few items and then build from there. Once you have a handful of listings under your belt, you'll be amazed at how listing becomes second nature!

Remember that first and foremost, you must utilize Etsy SEO to drive traffic to your shop. It all boils down to repeating the most important keywords in your titles, descriptions, tags, and shop sections. Master optimizing your listings before you consider whether you want to invest in *Etsy Ads*. And if you do decide to try *Etsy Ads*, start with a small budget of $5 per day. You may find, as I have, that you don't need to pay for advertising as your listings bring traffic in on their own. However, I encourage you to opt-into *Etsy Offsite Ads*, for which you only pay when an ad leads to a sale.

As you grow more comfortable running your Etsy shop, be sure to utilize social media to grow your business. Start with creating a *Facebook Page*, as it is still the best way to market an Etsy shop. Once your *Facebook Page* is up and running, consider expanding to other social media platforms, including Instagram and Twitter. If you enjoy making videos, TikTok and YouTube are also great places to showcase your shop.

And don't downplay the importance of networking with others in the "reselling community," which is particularly active on Instagram and YouTube. There are many other antique dealers online who love to talk about all things vintage. It's a very welcoming community that is always accepting of new sellers.

Finally, remember that while selling antiques is fun, you are also running a business. Be sure to track your numbers to ensure you are making a profit. Nothing is better than finding vintage treasures new homes while watching your bank account grow!

ABOUT THE AUTHOR

Ann Eckhart is a writer, entrepreneur, and online content creator based in Iowa. She has authored numerous books about home-based e-commerce businesses on topics including reselling, self-publishing, print-on-demand, and social media. You can find all her titles at www.AnnEckhart.com[1].

You can follow Ann Eckhart on the following social media platforms:

Facebook @anneckhart

Instagram @ann_marie_eckhart

YouTube @anneckhart

---

1. http://www.AnnEckhart.com

Don't miss out!

Visit the website below and you can sign up to receive emails whenever Ann Eckhart publishes a new book. There's no charge and no obligation.

https://books2read.com/r/B-A-UQFB-YGBTC

BOOKS 2 READ

Connecting independent readers to independent writers.

Also by Ann Eckhart

101 Items To Sell On Ebay
101 Items To Sell On Ebay
101 More Items To Sell On Ebay

2022 Home Based Business Books
Beginner's Guide To Amazon KDP 2022 Edition: How To Create &
Sell Books Using Kindle Direct Publishing
Beginner's Guide To Selling On Ebay 2022 Edition: How To Start &
Grow a Successful Online Reselling Business from Home
Beginner's Guide To YouTube 2022 Edition: How To Start & Grow a
Successful & Profitable YouTube Channel

2023 Home Based Business Books
Beginner's Guide To Selling On Ebay: 2023 Edition

Standalone
2020 Ebay Sourcing Guide
Ebay Seller Secrets

How to Start a YouTube Channel for Fun & Profit

Beginner's Guide To Amazon KDP: 2023 Edition

Beginner's Guide To Starting An Etsy Print-On-Demand Shop

Beginner's Guide To Starting An Etsy Sticker Shop

Beginner's Guide To WhatNot: How To Buy & Sell On The Live Auction Reselling App

Reseller Liquidation Database: The Top 35 Liquidation & Wholesale Companies for Online Sellers

2000+ Printable Products To Sell On Etsy

Beginner's Guide To Selling Digital Products On Etsy

Beginner's Guide To Amazon KDP 2024 Edition

Beginner's Guide To Selling Antiques On Etsy

Beginner's Guide To Selling Crafts On Etsy

Beginner's Guide To Selling On eBay 2024 Edition

Beginner's Guide To Starting a YouTube Channel 2024-2025 Edition

Watch for more at www.SeeAnnSave.com.